BRYONY'S COUNTRY KITCHEN

This book is dedicated to my late mother Bridget, whose wise guidance, patient instruction and frequent chiding helped me to fend for myself in the kitchen, knowing that I would always be in a position to put something on the table that was both nourishing and delicious

Dear David —

BRYONY'S COUNTRY KITCHEN

with huge gratitude

BRYONY HILL

Jan '23

Red Door

ACKNOWLEDGEMENTS

If it hadn't been for the patience, dedication and encouragement from the team at RedDoor Press namely Clare Christian and Heather Boisseau plus their design guru, indexer, proof reader et al, I would never have been able to complete another book. Thank you, everyone, for making this such an exciting and pleasurable experience and I apologise profusely for inundating you with so many last minute tweaks! You have succeeded in putting my words and ideas into truly beautiful books of which I am immensely proud.

A RedDoor book
Published by Ember Press 2022
www.emberprojects.co.uk
© 2022 Bryony Hill

Every effort has been made to trace copyright holders and to obtain their permission
for the use of copyright material. The author and publisher apologise for any errors
or omissions and would be grateful if notified of any corrections that should be
incorporated in future reprints or editions of this book

978-1-9997701-9-8

A CIP catalogue record for this book is available from the British Library

Cover design: Clare Connie Shepherd
Typesetting: Megan Sheer

Printed by Severn, Gloucester

CONTENTS

FOREWORD

Bryony's Country Kitchen makes me want to lie down. Not because I am tired, but because that's always been the best way first to enjoy a proper cookery book.

This *is* a proper cookery book, the way they were for centuries, just pages stuffed with anecdotes, tips and hints, and recipe after recipe we want to cook. But without silly micro-measurements and bullying colour plates.

Few of the most influential cookery books of the past centuries were lavishly illustrated. Think of the life-changing works of Elizabeth David, of Jane Grigson, Lady Arabella Boxer, Julia Child or James Beard – and Mrs Beeton or Hannah Glasse or Francatelli and hundreds of others before that. You might have thought that unillustrated books without exact measurements were the recipe for success. Yet for too many recent decades we have been intimidated by food mathematicians and by photographers and stylists, who usually earned more than the book's author.

Bryony's book headlines a return to cookery books that first make you want to snuggle down on a comfy sofa and then inspire you to get up and cook food that tastes and looks the way *you* want it to do. For me, first there's that Asparagus with Crunchy Peanut Butter, those guinea fowl ideas and the Sticky Toffee Pavlova ... and it's clear that a bit more or less of this or that will make no difference.

Thanks for thinking of us, Bryony.
Glynn Christian, 2022

Glynn Christian changed the world of delicatessen and ingredients with MR CHRISTIAN'S Provisions, opened in Portobello Road market in 1974. He went on to pioneer modern TV cookery on BBC *Breakfast Time* and helped found both the Guild of Food Writers and the Great Taste Awards. The author of many cookery books, his special interest is ingredients; REAL FLAVOURS was voted best food guide in the world and the latest version is *TASTE! How to Choose the Best Deli Ingredients* (Grub Street). Neither has colour plates.

His new *How to Crack The UK Employability Codes* is a guide to the aspirational young that includes codes for dress and social success, table manners, communication and grammar.

PROLOGUE

I have been busy in the kitchen for as long as I can remember, helping my mother from the moment I could stand to prepare meals, gather produce from our garden and compete with my two brothers to lick the bowl when baking cakes. Ma was a hands-on, stay-at-home mum who taught us to read and write (even though she suffered from dyslexia) before we went to school. With boundless patience, she also showed us how to weave baskets from cane, to make finger puppets from flour and water paste and, most importantly, how to cook.

In 1970, short of my nineteenth birthday, I left home for France to be companion/cook/housekeeper to a fourteen-year-old girl, her thirty-five-year-old brother and two dogs while their parents were on a cruise in the Caribbean. It was a rude awakening. A younger son was a student at Orléans University and the week after I landed on French soil, we paid him a visit. Sharing his apartment was a tall, ridiculously handsome, aristocratic Frenchman with whom I fell instantly in love. Mercifully, his parents accepted my presence in their beloved son and heir's life and who, on the occasions when we met up in Paris, treated me to some of the best meals in the best restaurants known to man. They taught me so much about food, what goes with what and how to enjoy the simplest of preparations with the minimum of fuss, encouraging the ingredients to speak for themselves. Up until then I had been more Gordon Bennett than Gordon Ramsay and finding myself confronted with myriad exotic and enigmatic dishes was exciting beyond belief. At these Pantagruelian feasts I savoured venison simmered with cherries in wine, tender, fried sweetbreads, ambrosial scrambled eggs studded with truffles and other dishes I would rather not have been told what they were after having consumed them.

My Frenchman whisked me away to the picturesque town of Honfleur on the Normandy coast and, for our first lunch, he ordered *tourteaux à la mayonnaise*: freshly cooked crab caught locally that morning near the mouth of the River Seine, accompanied by a bottle of chilled Muscadet sur Lie. The following summer his father booked tickets for us and our cocker spaniel puppy Ulla to travel overnight to the South of France on *Le Train Bleu*. Departing from La Gare de Lyon after a delicious supper at the eponymous restaurant within the station, the following morning the train hissed to a halt in Cannes in time for breakfast on the terrace of a café on the Croisette. A day or two later in nearby Saint-Raphaël I sampled *bouillabaisse*, the classic Mediterranean fish stew. So copious was the meal refreshed with liberal amounts of *rosé de Provence*, we crossed the square only to collapse on a pew in the neighbouring church, the cool ambience producing the deep sleep of the innocent, Ulla included.

Cooking is an art, a fascinating alchemic blending of ingredients, bringing together family and friends. Ask anyone who has experienced extreme happiness (or sadness) in their lives and I bet you a pound to a penny they will remember what they were eating at the time. One of those occasions for me was the first dinner *à deux* shared with my late husband Jimmy in the seventies. Having reserved a table in an Italian restaurant near my flat in Notting Hill he chose from the menu. Our starter was *speck*, a rustic dry, cured meat served with mayonnaise mixed with fresh herbs, the main a crunchy, deep-fried chicken Kiev (or chicken Kyiv, as it is now called) accompanied by a simple orange and onion salad followed not by a pudding but flaming sambucas.

Bryony's Country Kitchen is a compilation of meals I have prepared for myself since the publication of *Grow Happy, Cook Happy, Be Happy* in 2018. I am convinced that my honest, straightforward ideas could prove to be a godsend in households where the family may have multiple nutritional needs and preferences. The body needs variety to keep running on an even keel and, more by chance than design, many of the dishes are plant-based or vegetarian but there are plenty containing meat, poultry and fish.

You will notice that glossy, brightly coloured, carefully orchestrated photographs of oozing, golden egg yolks, one pot dishes and slow-cooked roasts are conspicuous by their absence. There is method in my madness. How many times have we attempted to replicate a dish the end result of which bears little or no resemblance to the adjacent image? By listing few ingredients with simple instructions these tasty, seasonal recipes are quick and easy to prepare even if you have little experience with a wooden spoon or whisk and, thus inspired, you will never feel you have failed. The best of British, happy cooking and above all, have fun.

MY STORE CUPBOARD STAPLES

ORGANIC IF POSSIBLE

* Low-calorie olive oil spray

* Extra virgin olive oil

* Everyday olive oil

* Sunflower oil

* Vegetable oil

* Vegetable and chicken jelly stock pots

* Marigold vegetable bouillon granules

* Frozen fish (of which I am a great believer): haddock and salmon, which can be cooked from frozen

* Tinned fish: tuna in brine, various sardines, anchovies

* Dark rye Ryvita

* Gram flour (made from chickpeas) which can thicken sauces, coat patties and be used to bind fritters and is gluten-free

* Organic free-range eggs

* Dark and light soy

* Toasted sesame oil

* Worcestershire sauce

* Tabasco sauce

* The best balsamic vinegar I can afford

* Unfiltered organic cider vinegar

* White and red wine vinegar

* Seeds such as pumpkin, sunflower, pine nuts and sesame

* Unwaxed lemons – buying organic only when I want to use the zest

* Sweetcorn in plain water – no sugar or salt added

* Tins or packets of various organic beans, pulses and chickpeas in water

* Fresh herbs: coriander, basil (Greek and sweet), dill, thyme, bay, parsley (flat leaf and curly), sage and rosemary – dried herbs are fine but you may need to adjust the quantities

* Sea salt (coarse and fine) and black peppercorns

* Spices: cumin (ground and whole), coriander (ground and whole), cardamom, turmeric, fennel seeds, ground ginger, cloves (ground and whole), celery salt, garam masala, cinnamon (sticks and ground)

* Good-quality curry powder

* Full-fat milk

* Natural, full-fat yoghurt

* Best quality mayonnaise

* Frozen petits pois

* Frozen baby broad beans

* Frozen North Atlantic cold-water prawns

* Varieties of pasta

* Dry rice and egg noodle nests

* Wholegrain rice and basmati – wild is expensive but wonderful for a special treat

* Dried pulses of all shapes and sizes: yellow, red and green lentils, beans, quinoa and any other grains which take your fancy

* Pouches of ready-to-use Puy and Beluga lentils, quinoa, etc. – wonderful time-savers

* Organic, reduced sugar baked beans

* Vegetables, vegetables and more vegetables, fresh and frozen

* Fruit: remember that the tropical varieties such as mango, melon, etc. contain more sugar. Interestingly, one kiwi fruit is richer in Vitamin C than an orange and provides you with almost your entire daily needs

* Frozen bags of different red fruits – perfect for an instant smoothie or gently stewed in their own juice to mix with natural yoghurt

* Nuts (unsalted): almonds, walnuts, cashews, etc. eaten as a nibble or chopped in salads or used as a topping for fish, chicken, etc.

* Jumbo porridge oats

* Medjool dates – high in sugar, yes, but full of nutritional value and best eaten on an empty tummy before breakfast for full benefits

* Dried ready-to-eat fruits such as untreated apricots, figs and prunes

* Proper pukka butter – it helps you absorb vital nutrients such as Vitamins A, E, D in sunshine and K

* A spiraliser

* A set of measuring spoons

TIPS

When cooking mushrooms, slice them finely and simmer gently in a little water and lemon juice, stirring every now and again. Once the liquid has evaporated the mushrooms will be cooked without using any fat or oil.

If you crave a sugar rush at teatime keep the butter in the fridge and spread a thin layer of runny honey onto hot toast. Eyes shut, you would never know it was flying solo.

Turkey is lower in fat than chicken and the breasts of both can be flattened between cling film to make fast-cooking escalopes or cut into strips for a stir fry.

If you want to make a fruit jelly, fresh kiwi or pineapple will prevent it from setting. Curiously tinned pineapple works perfectly.

Please forgive me in advance for not mentioning how many each recipe can feed. Generally the soups will be for two people and, as for the fish dishes, I calculate one fillet per person. When it comes to salads what I don't eat will generally keep for the next day.

Where I can I have marked the recipes which are vegetarian with a V, those which are vegan with a VG, those which are dairy-free with a DF and those which are gluten-free with a GF, but please check your own ingredients. Recipes containing aged cheeses (Parmesan, Cheddar cheese etc.) are not marked as vegetarian as many are made using animal rennet, but feel free to use a vegetarian option as you see fit.

Where I have inserted brackets the dairy content, i.e. milk, cream, crème fraîche, can be omitted and chicken stock can be substituted with vegetable stock or plain water.

MA'S TIPS

For my dear little dort when she leaves home and does her own housekeeping and cooking

HERBS

* Sweet cicely for fruits
* Angelica stalk for acid fruits
* Rosemary with mushroom
* Chervil – carrots and egg
* Add herbs to pastry mixture

* **Lemon juice on grated carrots:** heat some oil and add mustard seeds and pour over

* **Add a tablespoon of cornflour** to sugar for fruit pies to thicken the juices

* **Add full-fat, natural yoghurt** to a curry that's too hot

* **Turkey:** to heat up. Butter thickly some greaseproof paper (not foil). Put on turkey slices, more butter, fold over. In oven till the paper browns

* **Melting chocolate:** put into a polythene bag to melt over hot water. Cut off corner and squeeze out. OR: put in pan with cold water. When melted pour off water carefully

* **Mix grated lemon rind with breadcrumbs** for coating fish, etc.

* **Quick stuffing:** use packet of instant bread sauce, mix with sausage meat and add herbs and/or lemon zest

* **1 egg = 2oz**

* **Fresh fruit juice drink:** add pinch of citric acid to sharpen especially when glucose is added for invalids

* **Coal:** add washed lump to peeled potatoes to keep white

* **Freshen lettuce** with lemon rind in iced water

* **Onions:** to sweat put in a pan with butter and cover with damp greaseproof paper then lid. Will prevent browning

* **Eggs:** to remove a piece of shell, use one half of broken shell to lift it out

* **Pâté:** to test for seasoning, fry a little in butter, then taste

* **Martini Dry:** instead of white wine and only use half the amount

* **Put black olives in olive oil** that doesn't taste much of olives

* **Wine and cheese party quantities per person:** 3oz biscuits and 2 slices bread (20 people = 2 large loaves, 3–4lbs biscuits). 1lb butter = 40 pats. ½ bottle per head

SMOKED SALMON ROLLS

* 1 brown (large) sandwich loaf
* 1lb butter
* 1lb smoked salmon
* Makes 12 slices rolled

SKIN CLEANSER

* 6 tablespoons of elderflowers
* ½ pint milk
* Simmer 30 minutes, cover, leave 3 hours
* Strain. Store in fridge

BREAD

This is a power-packed bundle of yumminess.

MULTI-SEEDED BREAD TO BE COOKED IN A BREAD MACHINE

* 315g organic strong white flour
* 315g wholewheat seeded bread flour
* 25g rye flakes
* 50g wholegrain bulgar wheat
* 50g sunflower seeds
* 25g mixed red, black and white quinoa
* 25g organic porridge oats
* 2 teaspoons dry yeast
* 2 teaspoons salt
* 110ml warm water + one tablespoon extra mixed with:
* 110ml semi-skimmed milk

Put the ingredients in your bread machine (recipe for wholemeal bread) in the order in which they suggest. It will be a large loaf so make sure you set it accordingly with a medium colour setting. When cold, I slice it and put 4 slices in individual bags and freeze them.

SOUPS

There is no secret formula required to create a tasty bowl of soup: a delicate broth can be made quickly from water, a carrot, a leek, a pinch of chilli flakes (optional) and a potato. Blitz the vegetables once they are cooked, add a touch of milk for extra richness, season with salt and pepper and it's ready to eat in under half an hour. If handy, I use up any leftover vegetables from the day before and mix them with stock made from the carcass of a roast chicken, Marigold bouillon granules or jelly pots but, if using the latter, it is essential to taste the soup before adding any extra seasoning.

LEEK, GREEN PEPPER AND LETTUCE SOUP

 & (IF USING VEGETABLE STOCK) (IF OMITTING MILK)

* 1 leek, sliced
* 1 green pepper, deseeded and roughly chopped
* 1 little gem lettuce, sliced
* 500ml chicken/vegetable stock
* a little milk to taste – about 125ml

Put all in a saucepan (except the milk), bring to the boil, simmer and cook until the vegetables are soft. Blitz with a handheld blender, add the milk and season accordingly.

BROCCOLI, CELERY AND RED ONION SOUP

 & (IF USING VEGETABLE STOCK) (IF OMITTING MILK)

* 200g broccoli, roughly chopped
* 1 stick celery, sliced
* 1 red onion, roughly chopped
* pinch chilli flakes
* 500ml chicken/vegetable stock
* 150ml milk
* salt and freshly ground black pepper

Put everything into a saucepan except the milk, bring to the boil, stir and cover with a lid. Simmer on a gentle boil for about 10 minutes or until the vegetables are soft. Blitz in the pan with a handheld blender, add the milk and taste. Adjust seasoning with salt and pepper.

KALE AND VEGETABLE SOUP

* 200g kale
* 2 carrots, roughly chopped
* 1 leek, sliced
* 4 tomatoes, roughly chopped
* 2 tablespoons red lentils
* 1 vegetable jelly stock pot dissolved in 500ml boiling water

Put everything into a saucepan, bring to the boil and simmer until the lentils are cooked through. Blitz with a handheld blender and serve.

YELLOW LENTIL AND MIXED VEGETABLE SOUP

* 200g dried yellow lentils
* 1 aubergine (225g), roughly chopped
* 300g mix of green, red, yellow and/or orange peppers, deseeded and roughly chopped
* 1 stick celery, sliced
* 2 carrots, roughly chopped
* 2 leeks, sliced
* 1 red or green chilli, deseeded and finely sliced
* 1 sweet potato (250g), peeled and roughly chopped
* 1x 400g tin cherry tomatoes
* 1 teaspoon dried mixed herbs
* 1 red onion, roughly chopped
* 1 clove garlic, chopped
* 500ml vegetable stock

Cook the lentils in plenty of vegetable stock by bringing them up to the boil and cook at a high heat for 10 minutes. Reduce the heat and add all the other ingredients, plus more water if needed. Simmer gently until the lentils are soft. This soup is best kept lumpy. Serve with a sprinkling of parsley.

LEEK, SWEET POTATO AND CELERY SOUP

 & (IF USING VEGETABLE STOCK)

* 1 sweet potato (250g), peeled and roughly chopped
* 1 stick celery, sliced
* 2 leeks, sliced
* ½ green chilli, deseeded and finely sliced
* 500ml chicken/vegetable stock

All together in a pan, brought up to the boil and simmered for 10 minutes, then blitzed.

WINTER WARMER ROOT VEGETABLE SOUP

 &  (IF USING VEGETABLE STOCK AND OMITTING MILK) (IF OMITTING MILK)

* 4 carrots, roughly chopped
* 1 stick celery, sliced
* 1 onion, roughly chopped
* 1 sweet potato (250g), peeled and roughly chopped
* 1 clove garlic, chopped
* 1 tablespoon concentrated tomato purée
* 1 red chilli, deseeded and chopped
* 1 chicken/vegetable jelly stock pot
* water
* milk
* low-calorie olive oil spray

Put all the vegetables into a deep saucepan and add about 5 squirts of low-calorie olive oil spray. Stir and sweat for 3 minutes before adding the tomato purée and garlic and enough water to cover. Stir, bring to the boil, cover and simmer for about 15 minutes or until the vegetables are soft. Add about 275ml of milk and blitz. Check for seasoning and serve.

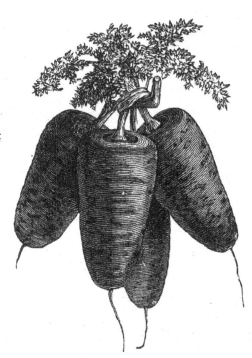

BEETROOT AND SWEET POTATO SOUP

 (IF USING VEGETABLE STOCK) (IF OMITTING MILK /CREAM)

* 2 raw beetroots, peeled and roughly chopped
* 1 stick celery, sliced
* 1 carrot, roughly chopped
* 100g watercress, well washed and roughly chopped
* 500ml chicken/vegetable stock

Put everything except the watercress in a pan, bring to the boil, cover and simmer until the vegetables are soft. Add the watercress, stir and cook for a further 5 minutes. Blitz with a handheld blender and decorate with a little chopped parsley and a swirl of milk or cream (optional).

SWEET POTATO, GREEN PEPPER AND PEA SOUP

(IF USING VEGETABLE STOCK) (IF USING VEGETABLE STOCK AND OMITTING MILK)

(IF OMITTING MILK)

* 1 green pepper, deseeded and roughly chopped
* 1 sweet potato (250g), peeled and roughly chopped into small pieces
* 300g frozen peas or petits pois
* 1 chicken/vegetable jelly stock pot
* 1 teaspoon olive oil (optional)
* 120ml milk

Put the green pepper and sweet potato in a saucepan with the olive oil, if using. Stir for a minute or two and add the jelly stock pot plus 500ml of water. Bring to the boil and simmer for about 8 minutes or until the vegetables are nearly cooked. Add the peas, bring back to the boil and cook a further 5 minutes. Blitz with a handheld blender and add the milk. Check for seasoning – you probably won't need to add any salt but a few grinds of black pepper will lift it.

ASPARAGUS, PEA SHOOT AND MINT SOUP

 & (IF USING VEGETABLE STOCK AND OMITTING MILK)   (IF OMITTING MILK)   (GF)

* 250g asparagus, trimmed and cut into 3cm pieces
* 250g frozen peas
* 30g fresh mint
* 1 chicken/vegetable jelly stock pot
* 150ml milk
* freshly ground black pepper
* dash of olive oil

Put the vegetables, mint and olive oil into a pan, stir and cook for 2 minutes before adding the jelly stock pot and about 450ml of boiling water. This won't take long to cook – about 8 minutes, and don't overdo it or you will spoil the fresh flavour. Blitz in the pan and add the milk. Check for seasoning – it probably won't need any extra salt because there will be plenty in the jelly stock pot.

CARROT, CORIANDER, LEEK AND ORANGE SOUP

(V) (VG) (IF OMITTING MILK)   (DF) (IF OMITTING MILK)   (GF)

* 2 large carrots, roughly chopped
* 1 leek, sliced
* juice 2 oranges
* 1 heaped teaspoon vegetable bouillon powder
* 1 teaspoon coriander seeds
* small handful (1 tablespoon) fresh coriander
* 150ml milk
* splash of olive oil
* freshly ground black pepper

Put the carrots and leek in a saucepan with a splash of olive oil. Stir and sweat for 3 minutes. Add the bouillon powder and about 425ml of water. Bring to the boil, cover and simmer for about 10 minutes or until the vegetables are soft. Heat a non-stick frying pan and dry roast the coriander seeds for a couple of minutes, shaking the pan to avoid burning. Tip into a pestle and mortar and pound to a fine dust. Add to the vegetables along with the orange juice and fresh coriander and blitz with a handheld blender. Stir in the milk and several grinds of black pepper.

ROASTED SWEDE, SWEET POTATO AND VEGETABLE SOUP WITH A DRIZZLE OF HONEY

 V & VG (IF USING VEGETABLE STOCK AND MAPLE SYRUP) DF (IF OMITTING MILK) GF

* 250g swede, peeled and roughly chopped
* 1 onion, cut into quarters
* 1 carrot, roughly chopped
* 1 stick celery, sliced
* 1 sweet potato (250g), peeled and roughly chopped
* 1–2 teaspoons runny honey or maple syrup
* 500ml hot chicken/vegetable stock (or plain water)
* 150ml milk
* olive oil
* salt and freshly ground black pepper

Preheat the oven to 180°C (fan). Place the vegetables on a shallow baking tray and drizzle with the olive oil and honey. Bake until the vegetables are soft and taking on a little colour. Put into a pan along with the hot stock and blitz with a handheld blender. Add the milk, whizz, taste and season accordingly, remembering that some stock cubes are saltier than others.

CLEAR CHICKEN AND TOMATO BROTH WITH WHOLEGRAIN RICE NOODLES

  DF GF

* 500ml chicken stock
* 6 tomatoes, roughly chopped
* 1 nest wholegrain rice noodles
* salt and freshly ground black pepper

Bring the stock and tomatoes to the boil, reduce the heat and simmer gently for about 8 minutes. In the meantime, cook the noodles according to pack instructions. Pass the soup through a sieve, squashing as much of the tomato pulp as possible. Drain the noodles and cut up into small pieces and add to the soup. Check for seasoning and serve.

GAZPACHO

* 450g ripe tomatoes
* 1 green pepper, deseeded and roughly chopped
* 1 red pepper, deseeded and roughly chopped
* 1 clove garlic, chopped
* 1 stick celery, sliced
* 4 spring onions, sliced
* 1 tablespoon extra virgin olive oil
* 1 tablespoon organic cider or sherry vinegar
* salt and freshly ground black pepper

Prick the tomatoes with the point of a knife and put them into a heatproof bowl and cover with boiling water. Leave for 3 minutes, drain and peel off the skin. Cut in half and add to the other vegetables. Blitz them with the olive oil and vinegar until smooth, taste and adjust the seasoning. You may need to slacken the soup with a little water. Pour into a container with a lid and chill in the fridge. Serve cold with garlic croutons or crispy French bread.

WINTER WARMER SOUP

 & (IF USING VEGETABLE STOCK AND OMITTING MILK)   (IF OMITTING THE CHEESE AND MILK)

* 1x 400g tin beans (cannellini, butter, haricot, chickpeas, etc.), drained and rinsed
* 250g green cabbage, sliced
* 1 onion, roughly chopped
* 2 carrots, roughly chopped
* 1 stick celery, sliced
* 1 clove garlic, chopped
* 1 tablespoon olive oil
* 1 fresh red chilli, deseeded and sliced or a pinch of dried chilli flakes
* 1x 400g tin chopped tomatoes
* ½ teaspoon sugar
* 500ml stock (chicken or vegetable)
* salt and pepper to taste
* 2 tablespoons grated Emmental cheese
* 1 tablespoon chopped parsley

Heat the olive oil in a saucepan and add the onion, carrots, celery, garlic and chilli. Stir and cook for a couple of minutes. Tip in the cabbage and stir for a further minute. Add the beans, tomatoes, sugar and stock. Bring to a gentle boil for about 10 minutes or until the vegetables are cooked. Season with salt and pepper. Serve with a sprinkle of parsley and a spoonful of the cheese, which will melt.

EMERGENCY SOUP

  (SEE BELOW)

* 1x 400g tin cream of mushroom soup (check on tin to see if gluten-free)
* 1x 400g tin pea soup
* 1x 400g soup tin milk
* 1x 400g soup tin water
* 1 onion, sliced
* cream (optional)

Put everything but the cream in a saucepan and heat to boiling point, stirring constantly. Simmer for about 6–8 minutes in order to cook the onion and serve with a swirl of cream (optional).

LETTUCE AND MINT SOUP

 & (IF USING VEGETABLE STOCK) (IF OMITTING CREAM AND BUTTER)

* 1 large potato, peeled and roughly chopped
* 1 onion, roughly chopped
* knob of butter (about a heaped teaspoon) or a splash of oil
* 500ml chicken/vegetable stock
* 2 little gem lettuces, washed and shredded
* small handful of mint, chopped
* salt and pepper
* cream (optional)
* 1 tablespoon chopped herbs such as parsley/chives

Heat the butter/oil in a pan and add the potato and onion. Cook for 5 minutes and add the stock. Bring to the boil and simmer until the vegetables are soft. Add the lettuce and mint and bring back to the boil for a further 2–3 minutes. Do not cover the pan. Whizz with stick blender, season with salt and pepper and decorate with a swirl of cream (optional) and the herbs.

SWEETCORN AND COURGETTE SOUP

 & (IF USING VEGETABLE STOCK) AND OMITTING MILK (IF OMITTING CREAM AND BUTTER)

* 1 fresh corn on the cob, outer husks removed or 1x 160g tin of unsweetened corn
* 1 teaspoon butter/oil
* 1 courgette, roughly chopped
* 1 medium onion, roughly chopped
* 1 stick celery, sliced
* 2 cloves garlic, chopped
* 500ml chicken/vegetable stock
* 275ml milk
* cream (optional)
* chopped parsley to decorate

Using a sharp knife, remove the corn kernels from the cob. Melt the butter or heat the oil in a pan and add the vegetables. Stir and cook for 5 minutes. Add the stock and bring to the boil. Simmer for about 5 minutes until the vegetables are soft. Whizz with a stick blender but leave a little texture. Season with salt and pepper and add the milk. Serve with a sprinkle of parsley and cream (optional).

CHEAT'S PRAWN BISQUE

 (IF OMITTING CREAM)

You will need to plan a few days ahead for this so that the chilli sherry has time to mature. Find a small bottle or jar with a lid and pour in a tablespoon or two of medium dry (Amontillado) sherry and add either a deseeded and chopped red chilli or a pinch of dried flakes. Leave on a sunny windowsill for two or three days, shaking it now and again.

* 175g prawns (thaw first if frozen)
* 1x 400g tin tomato soup
* 1x 400g tin lentil soup
* cream
* chilli sherry (see above)

Keep a few prawns to one side and lightly blitz the rest in a small blender. Put the soup into a pan with the prawns and heat gently to boiling point. Add a little of the chilli sherry and check for seasoning. When serving, place a couple of the whole prawns in each bowl before adding the hot soup, then decorate with a swirl of cream.

SALMOREJO SOUP

 (IF OMITTING HAM)

* 450g ripe tomatoes
* 1–2 slices multi-seeded bread, broken into small pieces
* 1 hard-boiled egg
* 110ml virgin olive oil
* 1 teaspoon sherry vinegar
* salt
* 1 clove garlic, chopped
* 1 teaspoon (per serving) finely chopped smoked ham

Put the tomatoes in a heatproof bowl and pierce with a pointed knife. Pour over a kettle of boiling water and leave for 2 minutes. Drain and rinse under the cold tap before peeling off the skins and removing the cores. Put into a blender and whizz till smooth. Add the bread and leave to soak for 5 minutes. Add the garlic, sherry vinegar, three-quarters of the hard-boiled egg and salt. Whizz till smooth and then add the olive oil until all is blended. Allow to chill in the fridge for several hours before serving with a sprinkle of the remaining egg, chopped finely, along with the ham.

COLD SHANNON SOUP

   GF

* 450g ripe tomatoes cut in half/quarters
* 1 fennel bulb, sliced
* 2 onions, roughly chopped
* 1 clove garlic, chopped
* small handful fresh basil leaves
* ½ teaspoon sugar
* 1 tablespoon olive oil
* juice ½ lemon
* vegetable stock
* Tabasco or hot chilli sauce
* salt and freshly ground black pepper

Preheat the oven to 180°C (fan). Put all the ingredients except the stock, lemon juice and Tabasco/chilli sauce into a shallow oven dish and roast for about 40–50 minutes or until they begin to take on a deep colour. Cool slightly and pass through a sieve. Measure the purée and add an equal amount of vegetable stock, the lemon juice and 3–4 drops of Tabasco or a teaspoon of chilli sauce. Mix well together and allow to chill thoroughly. This can be done the day before. Serve in small bowls with a sprinkle of chopped chives.

CARROT AND WATERCRESS SOUP

 & (IF USING VEGETABLE STOCK AND OMITTING MILK)   (IF OMITTING MILK)

* 4 carrots, roughly chopped
* 1 stick celery, sliced
* 100g watercress, thoroughly washed and roughly chopped
* 400ml chicken/vegetable stock or jelly pot
* 150ml milk
* pinch chilli flakes
* salt and freshly ground black pepper
* 1 teaspoon olive oil

Put the carrots and celery into a saucepan with the olive oil and sweat for 2–3 minutes. Add the chicken/vegetable stock and chilli flakes, stir and bring to the boil. Reduce the heat slightly and cook until the vegetables are soft. Add the watercress and bring back to the boil. Cook for a further 2 minutes, remove from the heat and blitz with a handheld blender. Add the milk, blitz again and check for seasoning.

CARROT AND GREEN PEPPER SOUP

 & (IF USING VEGETABLE STOCK) AND OMITTING MILK   (IF OMITTING MILK)

* 2 carrots, roughly chopped
* 1 green pepper, deseeded and roughly chopped
* 500ml chicken/vegetable stock
* splash of milk
* salt and freshly ground black pepper

Put the vegetables in a pan with the stock. Bring to the boil, reduce the heat and simmer for about 10 minutes or until soft. Blitz with a handheld blender, add a splash of milk and season accordingly.

CARROT AND ORANGE SOUP

 & (IF USING VEGETABLE STOCK) AND OMITTING MILK (IF OMITTING MILK) (GF)

* 10 baby carrots or 5 medium-sized carrots, roughly chopped
* 1 onion, roughly chopped
* 1 stick celery, sliced
* 500ml vegetable/chicken stock
* 1 teaspoon olive oil
* juice 1 orange
* 150ml milk
* salt and freshly ground black pepper

Sweat the vegetables in the olive oil for about 3 minutes, add the stock and bring to the boil. Cover and simmer for about 10 minutes or until the vegetables are cooked. Remove from the heat and blitz with a handheld blender. Add the orange juice, stir and season before adding the milk. Serve with a few fresh coriander leaves.

LEEK AND WATERCRESS SOUP

 & (IF USING VEGETABLE STOCK AND OMITTING MILK) (IF OMITTING MILK) (GF)

* 500ml chicken/vegetable stock
* 100g watercress, thoroughly washed
* 2 leeks, sliced
* salt and freshly ground black pepper
* splash of milk

Put the stock in a pan with the leeks, bring to the boil, stir and cover. Simmer for about 10 minutes before adding the watercress. Cook for a further 5 minutes then blitz in the pan with a handheld blender. Add the milk and check for seasoning.

ASPARAGUS, PEA SHOOT AND LETTUCE SOUP

  & (IF USING VEGETABLE STOCK AND OMITTING MILK) (IF OMITTING MILK)

* 250g asparagus, sliced
* 160g sugar snap peas, sliced
* 1 red onion, roughly chopped
* 1 whole lettuce of your choice or 120g mixed lettuce leaves
* 1 chicken/vegetable jelly stock pot
* 150ml milk
* salt and freshly ground black pepper
* 1 teaspoon olive oil

Put the olive oil into a medium-sized saucepan, add the asparagus and red onion. Sweat and stir for a minute or two, add the jelly stock pot and about 500ml of boiling water. Simmer for about 10 minutes then add the lettuce and pea shoots/sugar snap peas. Bring back to the boil and cook a further 5 minutes. Using a handheld blender, whizz until liquidised. Add the milk, whizz again, taste and season accordingly, remembering that the jelly stock pot will be quite salty.

LETTUCE AND MINT SOUP

   GF

* 1 medium-sized potato, peeled and roughly chopped
* 1 onion, roughly chopped
* 1 tablespoon olive oil
* 500ml vegetable stock
* 2 little gem lettuces, sliced
* small handful fresh mint
* salt and freshly ground black pepper

Sweat the potato and the onion in a pan with the olive oil for about 3 minutes. Add the stock, bring to the boil, cover and simmer for about 10 minutes or until the vegetables are soft. Add the lettuce and mint, bring back to the boil but do not replace the lid – this will keep the soup bright green. Cook for about 2 minutes, remove from the heat and whizz with a handheld blender. Serve either immediately or chilled with a sprinkle of chopped fresh herbs.

BEETROOT AND WATERCRESS SOUP

 &  (IF USING VEGETABLE STOCK AND OMITTING MILK) DF GF

* 1 raw beetroot, peeled and chopped
* 1 stick celery, sliced
* 1 leek, sliced
* 100g watercress, thoroughly washed
* 1 chicken/vegetable jelly stock pot
* 500ml water

Put all the vegetables except the
watercress into a saucepan with
the chicken stock and water. Stir
and bring to the boil. Simmer
for about 20 minutes or until
the beetroot is soft and then add
the watercress. Bring back to the boil and
cook for a minute or two. Blitz with a
handheld blender and check for seasoning,
remembering that the jelly stock pot is already
salted.

AVOCADO, CUCUMBER AND MINT SOUP

 & (IF USING VEGETABLE STOCK) GF

* 275ml chicken/vegetable stock, cooled
* 1 ripe avocado
* ½ cucumber, peeled and finely chopped
* 2 tablespoons natural yoghurt
* juice ½ lemon
* salt and freshly ground black pepper

Add the vegetables to the stock and blitz till smooth in a liquidiser or using a handheld
blender. Add the lemon juice and season accordingly. Serve chilled.

WATERCRESS, LEEK AND ASPARAGUS SOUP

 & (IF USING VEGETABLE STOCK AND OMITTING MILK) (IF OMITTING MILK) (GF)

* 110g watercress
* 1 leek, sliced
* 125g asparagus tips
* 1 chicken/vegetable jelly stock pot
* 150ml milk

Put the leek and asparagus into a saucepan with the jelly stock pot and about 450ml of water; bring to the boil and simmer for 6 minutes. Thoroughly wash the watercress and roughly chop before adding it to the other vegetables. Stir and cook for a further 3 minutes. Remove from the heat, blitz with a handheld blender then pour in about a cupful of milk. Blitz again and check for seasoning, remembering the jelly stock pot will already contain salt. This was a lovely soup when served hot and I had some left over, which I chilled in the fridge overnight. I tasted it and, rather than reheat it, I enjoyed it cold almost more than when hot. Perfect for a summer's lunch in the garden. Think Vichyssoise.

CREAM OF CUCUMBER, SWEET POTATO, CELERY AND ONION SOUP

 & (IF USING VEGETABLE STOCK AND OMITTING MILK) (IF OMITTING THE MILK)

* ½ cucumber, roughly chopped
* 6–8 spring onions, sliced
* 1 sweet potato (250g), peeled and roughly chopped
* 1 stick celery, sliced
* 1 clove garlic, chopped
* 1 chicken/vegetable jelly stock pot/cube
* 150ml milk
* 1 tablespoon olive oil

Put all the vegetables into a large saucepan along with the olive oil. Stir and sweat for about 5 minutes. Add the jelly stock pot/cube and about 450ml of water. Bring to the boil, reduce heat and simmer till soft – about 10 minutes. Blitz with a handheld blender, add the milk and whizz again. Taste and adjust seasoning accordingly.

MANGETOUT, MINT AND VEGETABLE SOUP

 & (IF USING VEGETABLE STOCK AND OMITTING MILK) (IF OMITTING MILK)

* 160g either mangetout or sugar snap peas or 100g frozen peas
* 1 leek, sliced
* 1 carrot, roughly chopped
* 1 stick celery, sliced
* 1 chicken/vegetable jelly stock pot
* 1 tablespoon mint, roughly chopped
* 275ml milk

Put everything in a pan except the mint and milk and just cover with water. Bring to the boil, stir, cover and simmer for about 8 minutes. Add the mint and continue cooking a further 3–5 minutes. Add the milk and blitz with a handheld blender. Check for seasoning and adjust accordingly, remembering that the jelly stock pot will be salty.

PARSLEY AND SWISS CHARD SOUP

 & (IF USING VEGETABLE STOCK AND OMITTING MILK) (IF OMITTING MILK)

* 1 stick celery, sliced
* 1 onion, roughly chopped
* 1 potato (175g), peeled and roughly chopped
* handful flat-leafed parsley, roughly chopped
* 200g Swiss chard, roughly chopped
* 1 chicken/vegetable jelly stock pot
* 1 tablespoon olive oil
* 150ml milk

Heat the oil in a saucepan and add the onions, potato and celery. Stir and cook for about 5 minutes. Add the Swiss chard, parsley and jelly stock pot and enough water (about 425ml) to cover the vegetables. Stir, bring to the boil and simmer for about 15 minutes. Allow to cool slightly and blitz with a handheld blender. Add the milk, blitz again and check for seasoning. Serve either hot or chilled with croutons.

SWEETCORN, TOMATO AND CELERY SOUP

 & (IF USING VEGETABLE STOCK AND OMITTING MILK) (IF OMITTING MILK) (GF)

* 1 large corn cob, outer husks discarded and kernels stripped
* 4 ripe tomatoes, roughly chopped
* 1 onion, roughly finely
* 1 stick celery, sliced
* 1 clove garlic, peeled and chopped
* 1 chicken/vegetable jelly stock pot
* water
* 150ml milk
* pepper
* 1 tablespoon olive oil

Heat a tablespoon of olive oil in a saucepan, add the vegetables and sweat for 5 minutes, stirring every now and again. Add the chicken/vegetable stock and about 500ml of water. Bring to the boil, cover and simmer for about 15 minutes or until the vegetables are soft. Blitz with a handheld blender and add the milk. Blitz again, check for seasoning and adjust remembering that the stock will already be salted.

SWIS,S CHARD, TOMATO AND CHILLI SOUP

 & (IF USING VEGETABLE STOCK)

* 200g Swiss chard, roughly chopped
* 1 red onion, roughly chopped
* 1 clove garlic, chopped
* 1 stick celery, sliced
* 4 ripe tomatoes, roughly chopped
* 1 chilli of your choice, deseeded and finely sliced
* 1 tablespoon olive oil
* chicken/vegetable jelly stock pot

Sweat the onion in a saucepan with about 1 tablespoon of olive oil and add all the other vegetables. Stir and cook for 3 minutes before adding the jelly stock pot and about 1 pint of water. Bring to the boil and simmer for about 10 minutes or until the vegetables are cooked. Don't overdo this or you will lose the fresh flavour. Blitz with a handheld blender and check for seasoning.

CUCUMBER, CELERY, LEEK AND GREEN PEPPER SOUP

 & (IF USING VEGETABLE STOCK AND OMITTING MILK) (IF OMITTING THE MILK) (GF)

* ½ cucumber, peeled and roughly chopped
* 1 stick celery, sliced
* 1 leek, sliced
* 1 green pepper, deseeded and roughly chopped
* 1 clove garlic, chopped
* 1 chicken/vegetable jelly stock pot
* 1 tablespoon olive oil
* 150ml milk (optional)

Put the vegetables into a saucepan with the olive oil and sweat for about 3 minutes, stirring every now and again. Add the chicken stock and about 450ml of water. Stir, bring to the boil and simmer for about 10–15 minutes or until everything is soft. Blitz in the pan with a handheld blender, check for seasoning and add a dash of milk if wanted.

TOMATO AND AUBERGINE SOUP

 & (IF USING VEGETABLE STOCK)

* 400g ripe tomatoes
* 1 aubergine (225g), roughly chopped
* 1 onion, roughly chopped
* 1 stick celery, sliced
* chilli of your choice, deseeded and sliced
* 500ml chicken/vegetable stock
* ¼ teaspoon sugar
* olive oil
* salt and freshly ground black pepper

Prick the tomatoes with a sharp knife and place in a heatproof bowl and cover with boiling water for 3 minutes. Drain and cool under the cold tap before peeling away the skins. Chop roughly. Heat a little oil in a saucepan and add the vegetables. Stir and sweat for 3 minutes before adding the sugar and chicken stock. Bring to the boil and simmer for about 10 minutes or until the vegetables are cooked. Blitz with a handheld blender and check for seasoning. Serve with a drizzle of olive oil.

CONCENTRATED ROASTED ROOT VEGETABLE AND TOMATO SOUP

 & (IF USING VEGETABLE STOCK)

* 3 red beetroots (or a mix of colours), peeled and roughly chopped
* 4 carrots, roughly chopped
* 1 red onion, roughly chopped
* 1 red pepper, deseeded and roughly chopped
* 2 small chillies, deseeded and cut in half
* 1 stick celery, sliced
* 1 clove garlic (optional. If the soup is to be frozen, don't add garlic now – add it later when you are going to eat it)
* 4 tomatoes, cut into quarters
* good drizzle of olive oil
* light seasoning of salt and pepper before roasting
* 1 chicken/vegetable jelly stock pot

Preheat the oven to 180°C (fan). Put all the vegetables on to a shallow oven tray, drizzle with olive oil and season lightly. Roast until the vegetables are soft and just beginning to blacken on the edge. Put the roasted vegetables into a saucepan with the jelly stock pot and about 500ml of boiling water. Bring back to the boil and simmer for about 5 minutes. Blitz with a handheld blender and check for seasoning.

LEEK, LETTUCE, TOMATO AND WHOLEGRAIN RICE NOODLE BROTH

 & (IF USING VEGETABLE STOCK)

* 1 leek, finely sliced
* 2 tomatoes
* 1 little gem lettuce, sliced
* 1 nest of wholegrain rice noodles
* 500ml chicken/vegetable stock
* 1 small chilli, deseeded and finely sliced or pinch of dried chilli flakes (optional)
* olive oil
* salt and freshly ground black pepper

Prick the tomatoes once or twice with the point of a knife and put them into a heatproof bowl. Pour boiling water over them to cover and leave for 2 minutes. Drain, refresh under the cold tap and peel off the skin. Remove the core and roughly chop. Put about 1 teaspoon of olive oil into a saucepan and add the lettuce, leek and tomatoes and chilli if using. Stir and sweat for a minute. Pour in the stock, bring to the boil and simmer until the vegetables are cooked – about 6–8 minutes. Add the nest of rice noodles, breaking them into smallish pieces, stir and leave to sit for about 4 minutes. Check for seasoning and serve in small bowls.

CONCENTRATED ROASTED VEGETABLES AS A BASE FOR SOUP OR (UNDILUTED) AS A SAUCE FOR PASTA

 & (IF USING VEGETABLE STOCK)

* 400g ripe tomatoes, cut in half or quarters
* 400g sweet potatoes, peeled and roughly chopped
* 1 red onion, roughly chopped
* 250g celeriac, peeled and roughly chopped
* 2 tablespoons olive oil
* ½ teaspoon sea salt

Preheat the oven to 180°C (fan). Place everything on to a shallow baking tray and roast until the vegetables are just beginning to singe. Cool and blitz, adding a little water to slacken the mixture. When cool, pack into small containers and freeze. Once frozen, remove from the containers and put into freezer bags, taking 1 or 2 out at a time either to use as a sauce for pasta or to dilute with stock (vegetable or chicken) to make a soup. Garlic can be added at this moment if required.

CREAM OF CARROT AND CELERY SOUP

 & (IF USING VEGETABLE STOCK AND OMITTING MILK) (IF OMITTING MILK)

* 425g chicken/vegetable stock
* 2 carrots, roughly chopped
* 1 stick celery, roughly chopped
* 150ml milk
* salt and pepper
* olive oil

Roughly chop the carrots and celery and put in a saucepan with a teaspoon of olive oil. Stir and sweat for 2 minutes. Add the stock, bring to the boil, reduce the heat and simmer for about 10–15 minutes or until the vegetables are soft. Blitz with a handheld blender and add enough milk to make it creamy. Check for seasoning and serve with a sprinkle of fresh herbs, such as parsley, chives, mint.

CREAM OF CAULIFLOWER AND MINT SOUP

(V) & (VG) (IF USING VEGETABLE STOCK AND OMITTING MILK) (DF) (IF OMITTING MILK) (GF)

* 400g cauliflower, roughly chopped
* 1 red onion, roughly chopped
* 1 stick celery, sliced
* 1 chicken/vegetable jelly stock pot
* 275ml milk
* 6–8 fresh mint leaves
* salt and freshly ground black pepper to taste
* 1 teaspoon olive oil

Sweat the onion, celery and cauliflower in a saucepan with the olive oil for about 4 minutes, stirring very frequently. Add the chicken jelly stock pot and about 450–600ml of water. Stir, bring to the boil, cover and reduce heat slightly. Cook until the vegetables are soft then blitz with a handheld blender. Add the mint leaves and the milk, blitz again and check for seasoning. Serve with a sprinkle more of fresh mint and a tiny drizzle of olive oil.

CREAM OF MUSHROOM SOUP

(VG) (IF USING VEGETABLE STOCK AND OMITTING CREME FRAICHE) (DF) (IF OMITTING CRÈME FRAÎCHE)

* 250g chestnut mushrooms, roughly chopped
* 1 onion, roughly chopped
* 1 stick celery, sliced
* 500ml chicken/vegetable stock
* 1 tablespoon crème fraîche
* salt and freshly ground pepper
* 1 teaspoon olive oil

Put the olive oil, celery and onion in a pan and sweat for 2 minutes. Add the stock, bring to the boil and simmer for about 5 minutes. Add the mushrooms and cook for a further 5 minutes. Remove from the heat and blitz with a handheld blender. Check for seasoning and adjust accordingly before whizzing in the crème fraîche. Serve with a sprinkling of chopped chives.

BUTTERNUT AND GINGER SOUP

 & (IF USING VEGETABLE STOCK, OIL INSTEAD OF BUTTER AND OMITTING MILK)   (IF USING OIL)

This is a lovely warming soup and the hint of ginger and chilli gives it extra oomph. It will serve 2 people generously.

* 500g butternut squash, peeled, any seeds and fibre removed, roughly chopped
* 5cm piece fresh root ginger, peeled and grated
* 1 clove garlic, chopped (optional)
* 1 onion, roughly chopped
* 1 stick celery, sliced
* pinch dried chilli flakes
* 1 dessertspoon butter/oil
* 600ml chicken/vegetable stock, or made with vegetable bouillon granules
* salt and pepper to taste (the stock will already be seasoned)
* 100ml milk

Melt the butter or heat the oil in a large pan and add the onion, celery, garlic, ginger and chilli flakes. Stir for a minute or two before adding the butternut. Add the stock, bring to the boil and simmer for about 15 minutes or until the vegetables are soft. Blitz with a stick blender, add the milk and check for seasoning.

BUTTERNUT, LEEK AND GREEN PEPPER SOUP

 (IF USING VEGETABLE STOCK)   (IF USING OIL AND VEGETABLE STOCK AND OMITTING MILK)

* 2 leeks, sliced
* 1 green pepper, deseeded and roughly chopped
* 250g butternut squash (from the straight end), peeled and roughly chopped
* 500ml water
* 1 chicken/vegetable jelly stock pot
* 1 clove garlic (optional), chopped
* knob of butter/1 tablespoon oil
* 150ml milk

Put all the vegetables into a saucepan with the butter or oil and sweat for a couple of minutes. Add the jelly stock pot and water and bring to the boil. Stir and simmer for about 15 minutes or until the vegetables are soft. Blitz with a handheld blender, add the milk and blitz again. Taste and adjust seasoning if necessary.

ALTERNATIVE BUTTERNUT SOUP

 (IF USING VEGETABLE STOCK)   (IF USING VEGETABLE STOCK, OIL AND OMITTING MILK) (GF)

* 250g butternut squash cut from the neck, peeled and roughly chopped
* 2 carrots, roughly chopped
* 1 large clove garlic, chopped
* 2 leeks, sliced
* knob butter/oil
* 600ml chicken/vegetable stock
* 100ml milk
* salt and pepper to taste

Melt the butter or heat the oil in a pan and add the vegetables. Stir and cook for 2–3 minutes before adding the stock. Bring to the boil and simmer until the vegetables are soft. Using a potato masher, crush the vegetables but not to a purée, add the milk, stir and taste adding salt if necessary and a couple of grinds of pepper. When ready to serve, sprinkle a few chopped celery leaves in each bowl.

CELERIAC SOUP

 & (IF USING VEGETABLE STOCK AND OMITTING MILK)

* 250g celeriac, peeled and roughly chopped
* 1 leek, sliced
* 100g watercress
* 400ml chicken/vegetable stock
* 275ml milk
* salt and pepper
* 1 tablespoon olive oil

Sweat the vegetables in the olive oil for 2–3 minutes and add the stock. Bring to the boil and simmer for about 10 minutes, or until the vegetables are cooked. Blitz with a handheld blender, add the milk, whizz again and check for seasoning.

SALADS

ORANGE, OLIVE AND RAISIN SALAD

* 6 oranges
* ½ jar pitted black olives
* 1 heaped tablespoon seedless raisins

DRESSING:

* 2 tablespoons olive oil
* 1 tablespoon dry sherry
* 1 tablespoon chopped mint
* 2–3 sprigs thyme, the leaves stripped

Remove the zest from one of the oranges with a vegetable peeler trying not to cut into the pith. Slice into very fine strips and blanch for a couple of minutes in boiling water. Drain and cool. Remove the peel from the remaining oranges and the pith from the first one. Slice and pick out any pips. Put into a pretty bowl and add the olives and raisins. Make the dressing by combining the ingredients in a jar. Shake well and pour onto the oranges etc. Stir and chill before serving.

ORANGE SALAD

This goes well as a side dish with roast duckling or goose.

* 1 orange per person, all the skin and pith removed with a sharp knife
* splash brandy
* 1 tablespoon oil of your choice
* 1 teaspoon caster sugar
* 1 teaspoon finely chopped chervil (this has a light aniseed flavour) or tarragon

Cut between the orange sections and remove the segments and place on to a pretty dish. Mix the oil with the brandy and sugar and pour over the orange pieces. Sprinkle with the fresh herbs and serve.

CUCUMBER SALAD

* 1 cucumber, peeled and thinly sliced
* 200ml crème fraîche
* 1 tablespoon white wine vinegar
* salt and pepper

Place the cucumber slices in a sieve over a bowl and sprinkle with a teaspoon of salt. Cover and leave for about an hour. Rinse thoroughly and dry in a clean drying-up towel, squeezing out as much water as possible. Mix the crème fraîche with the vinegar and mix with the cucumber. Check for seasoning and add salt and pepper to taste.

RICE SALAD

This is best prepared the day you wish to eat it because bacteria can develop quickly in cooked rice and don't bode well for happy tummies.

* 175g uncooked rice
* 110ml vegetable/sunflower oil
* salt and pepper
* 80ml white wine vinegar
* 1 green pepper, deseeded and roughly chopped
* 1 red apple, cored and chopped
* 3 spring onions, sliced
* 1 clove garlic, chopped
* ½ teaspoon curry powder
* 60g cashew nuts, roughly chopped
* 2 tablespoons raisins
* 2 tablespoons sultanas
* 2 tablespoons parsley, chopped

Cook the rice according to pack instructions. Drain and rinse in cold water. In a bowl, whisk the oil, salt, pepper and vinegar and add to the other ingredients. Mix well and serve with cold meats and other salads. Great barbecue food.

GRIDDLED ASPARAGUS, BROAD BEAN, RADISH AND TOMATO SALAD

 & (IF OMITTING PARMESAN)   (IF OMITTING THE PARMESAN)

* 250g asparagus, trimmed
* 4–6 cherry tomatoes, halved or quartered
* 200g frozen broad beans, lightly cooked and the skins removed
* juice ½ lemon
* 4 radishes, washed, trimmed and sliced
* 1 teaspoon balsamic vinegar
* 2 teaspoons olive oil
* scattering of Greek basil leaves
* 30g shavings Parmesan using a vegetable peeler
* salt and pepper

Cook the asparagus spears in a little boiling water for 3 minutes, remove from heat, drain and lightly coat with olive oil. Heat a griddle pan and finish cooking the asparagus, 2 minutes on each side. Boil the broad beans for 3 minutes, remove from heat and cool under the cold tap. Remove the outer skins and place on a pretty plate, the asparagus on top. Scatter the tomatoes and radishes, dot with shavings of Parmesan and squeeze over the lemon juice. Sprinkle the balsamic vinegar, season with salt and freshly ground black pepper and scatter the basil leaves. Serve at room temperature.

BUCKWHEAT SALAD

* 350g buckwheat, cooked according to pack instructions
* 1 large carrot, grated
* ½ cucumber, roughly chopped
* 1 stick celery, sliced
* 4 spring onions, sliced
* 6 cherry tomatoes, cut in half
* handful fresh parsley and mint

DRESSING:

* 1 heaped tablespoon yoghurt
* juice ½ lemon
* salt and freshly ground black pepper

Mix all the salad ingredients in a pretty bowl. Whisk the dressing ingredients together and gently fold into the salad ingredients and serve.

MIXED SALAD

* 1 endive, sliced
* 1x 400g tin chickpeas, drained and rinsed
* 1 apple, chopped into small pieces
* 3 spring onions, sliced
* 1 red onion, finely sliced
* 50g walnuts, broken into small pieces

DRESSING:

* juice ½ lemon
* 1 tablespoon good mayonnaise
* 1 tablespoon natural yoghurt
* salt and freshly ground black pepper

Mix all the salad ingredients and stir in the dressing. This will keep a day or so in the fridge.

RED CABBAGE, FENNEL AND SOFT-BOILED EGG SALAD

* 1 soft-boiled egg
* 250g red cabbage, finely shredded
* 1 fennel bulb, sliced
* 4 spring onions, sliced
* 1 stick celery, sliced
* 1 tablespoon sunflower seeds
* 1 tablespoon pumpkin seeds
* 1 red endive, sliced
* ½ yellow pepper, deseeded and sliced
* cress

DRESSING:

* 1 teaspoon tahini
* juice ½ lemon
* 1 tablespoon natural yoghurt
* salt and pepper

Assemble all the salad ingredients in a bowl and mix in the dressing. Serve with the soft-boiled egg peeled and cut in half on top and a sprinkling of cress.

SAVOURY EGG SALAD

* 1 hard-boiled egg per person
* 1 little gem lettuce, torn into pieces
* tomatoes, sliced
* 5 radishes, washed, trimmed and sliced
* handful parsley, roughly chopped
* 1 tablespoon mayonnaise
* 1 tablespoon extra virgin olive oil
* 2 teaspoons cider vinegar
* pinch celery salt
* salt and freshly ground black pepper

Cut the egg in half and scoop out the hard yolk and put it into a small dish. Mash it with the celery salt and mayonnaise plus a little black pepper. Spoon back into the egg white and place these on top of the torn lettuce, sliced radishes and tomatoes. Drizzle with the olive oil, cider vinegar and torn parsley leaves. Eat in the garden in summer sunshine.

BLACK BEAN, WHOLEGRAIN WILD RICE, TOMATO AND GREEN PEPPER SALAD

* 1x 400g tin black beans, drained and rinsed
* 150g wholegrain rice
* 1 tablespoon vegetable or sunflower oil
* 2 tomatoes, roughly chopped
* ½ green pepper, deseeded and chopped
* 1 red onion, finely sliced
* juice 1 lemon
* pinch ground coriander
* pinch ground cumin
* a little olive oil
* 1 clove garlic, crushed

Cook the rice according to the pack instructions. Allow to cool. In a non-stick pan add a little vegetable or sunflower oil then tip in the onion. Stir and add 3 tablespoons of water. When the water has evaporated, the onion is soft and taking on a little colour add the garlic, ground cumin and ground coriander. Stir for a minute, remove from the heat and add the lemon juice. Mix all the ingredients together and chill until needed.

LENTIL SALAD

* 1 pouch ready-cooked Puy lentils
* 1 stick celery, sliced
* ½ green pepper, deseeded and sliced
* 2 spring onions, finely sliced
* juice ½ lemon
* 1 tablespoon good mayonnaise
* 1 tablespoon crème fraîche
* 1 tablespoon each parsley and basil plus a few mint leaves, all finely chopped
* freshly ground black pepper

Mix everything together and serve in a pretty bowl.

RED CABBAGE, CELERIAC, BEETROOT AND FENNEL SALAD

* 500g red cabbage, finely sliced
* 250g celeriac, peeled and grated
* 1 fennel bulb, sliced
* 1 red onion or 2 red salad onions, sliced
* 1 tablespoon sunflower seeds
* 1 tablespoon pumpkin seeds
* handful parsley, roughly chopped
* juice 1 lemon
* 2 tablespoons natural yoghurt
* 1 tablespoon olive oil
* 1 dessertpoon unfiltered cider vinegar
* salt and pepper

Mix everything together and serve in a pretty bowl.

MIXED GRAIN TABBOULEH WITH AVOCADO

* 200g dried mixed grains (I used Lupe Organic, available at most supermarkets)
* ½ cucumber, roughly chopped
* 200g baby leeks
* 2 tomatoes, roughly chopped
* 1 avocado, sliced
* good handful mixed herbs: parsley, basil and mint
* juice 1 lemon
* olive oil to taste
* salt and freshly ground black pepper

Cook the grains according to the pack instructions. Heat a griddle or frying pan, add a little oil and cook the leeks turning every now and again until they are soft – about 6 minutes. Drain the grains, rinse under a cold tap and put in a bowl along with the cucumber, tomatoes and herbs. Allow the leeks to cool and then cut into small slices before adding to the rest. Add the lemon juice and olive oil and season to taste. Serve the avocado sliced on top.

CHUNKY JEWELLED SALAD

 & (IF OMITTING THE EGG AND YOGHURT)

* ½ cucumber, roughly chopped
* 1 hard-boiled egg
* 4 cherry tomatoes, cut into quarters
* 2 cooked beetroots, roughly chopped
* ½ green pepper, deseeded and roughly chopped
* 1 small kohlrabi or turnip, peeled and grated, or 6–8 radishes, washed, trimmed and sliced
* 100g handful cooked French beans, roughly sliced
* 1 red onion, finely sliced
* 1 red chicory, sliced
* 80g watercress, thoroughly washed and torn
* small handful flat-leafed parsley, roughly chopped
* 1 tablespoon natural yoghurt
* 1 tablespoon olive oil
* juice ½ lemon
* salt and freshly ground black pepper

Place all the vegetables in a dish and roughly mix. Top with the halved hard-boiled egg and the dressing made from the yoghurt, olive oil, lemon juice and seasoning.

MIXED SPROUTING SEEDS AND RADISH SALAD

* 100g sprouting mixed bean sprouts
* 100g sprouting alfalfa
* 10 radishes, washed, trimmed and sliced
* ½ cucumber, roughly chopped
* 1 tablespoon mixed sunflower and pumpkin seeds
* 2 tomatoes, roughly chopped
* 3 spring onions, sliced
* 1 tablespoon natural yoghurt
* juice 1 lemon
* 1 tablespoon olive oil
* salt and freshly ground black pepper

Wash the sprouting seeds and drain. Mix with all the other ingredients and serve. This will keep a day or two in the fridge.

ROOT VEGETABLE SLAW

* 250g celeriac, peeled and grated
* 1 carrot, grated
* 1 red onion, finely sliced
* 1 kohlrabi (or baby turnip), peeled and spiralised or grated
* 1 raw pink and white striped 'chioggia' (or red) beetroot, peeled and spiralised or grated
* 6 radishes, washed, trimmed and sliced
* 1 tablespoon sunflower seeds
* 1 tablespoon pumpkin seeds
* 1 teaspoon Dijon mustard
* juice ½ lemon
* 1 tablespoon good mayonnaise
* 1 tablespoon natural yoghurt
* a little salt and several grinds black pepper
* parsley

Mix everything together and serve with a sprinkle of parsley. For added protein, include a hard-boiled egg or some crumbled feta.

PURPLE CARROT, PURPLE KOHLRABI, CUCUMBER, AVOCADO, FETA AND SEED SALAD

V GF

* 2 purple carrots (if available) or orange, grated
* 1 purple kohlrabi or baby turnip, peeled and grated
* ½ cucumber, peeled and grated
* 3 spring onions, sliced
* 1 tablespoon mixed pumpkin and sunflower seeds
* 1 teaspoon finely ground flax and soya seeds (optional)
* 75g (vegetarian) feta, crumbled
* 1 avocado, sliced
* 6 cherry tomatoes, cut in half
* 120g mixed salad leaves
* 1 tablespoon natural yoghurt
* 1 tablespoon virgin olive oil
* 1 tablespoon red or white wine or cider vinegar
* juice 1 lemon
* salt and freshly ground black pepper

Mix the vegetables (except the avocado, tomatoes and salad leaves) and feta together with the yoghurt, olive oil, lemon juice, vinegar and seasoning and put in a pretty dish. Decorate with the sliced avocado, cherry tomatoes and salad leaves.

HERITAGE TOMATO AND MOZZARELLA SALAD

V GF

* selection different tomatoes, heritage or otherwise, sliced
* 1 (vegetarian) buffalo mozzarella, roughly torn
* handful fresh herbs: flat-leafed parsley, chives and Greek or sweet basil
* 2 tablespoons virgin olive oil
* 1 tablespoon sherry vinegar (or vinegar of your choice)
* salt and freshly ground black pepper

Arrange the tomatoes on a plate and strew with the mozzarella and herbs. Drizzle over the olive oil and vinegar and season well. Best served at room temperature soon after assembling.

MIXED BEAN, CORN AND CHICKPEA SALAD

* 1x 260g tin sweetcorn, drained
* 1x 400g tin chickpeas, drained and rinsed
* 1x 400g tin red kidney beans, drained and rinsed
* 1 red onion, finely chopped
* ½ red pepper, deseeded and chopped
* ½ yellow or orange pepper, deseeded and chopped
* 10 radishes, washed, trimmed and sliced
* 2 tablespoons olive oil
* 1 tablespoon cider vinegar
* salt and freshly ground black pepper

Mix everything together and serve. Keeps well for a day or two in the fridge. Chopped parsley, basil and/or chives can be added at the last moment.

PURPLE PROSE SALAD

  & (IF OMITTING THE FETA CHEESE) GF

* 1 purple kohlrabi, peeled and spiralised (or 100g finely sliced red cabbage)
* 1 carrot, spiralised or grated
* 1 fennel bulb, sliced
* ½ cucumber, spiralised or sliced
* 1 red salad onion or 4 spring onions, sliced
* 6 radishes, washed, trimmed and sliced
* 50g fresh microgreens of your choice or cress
* 1 cooked beetroot, peeled and roughly chopped
* 1 tablespoon mixed pumpkin and sunflower seeds
* 2 tablespoons olive oil
* 1 tablespoon red wine/cider vinegar
* salt and freshly ground black pepper
* 75g (vegetarian) crumbled feta

Mix all the vegetables and seeds together with the olive oil and vinegar, season well and decorate with the microgreens and crumbled feta.

MIXED SALAD WITH SEEDS

 (IF OMITTING THE YOGHURT)

* 1 small kohlrabi or baby turnip, peeled and grated or spiralised
* 1 carrot, grated or spiralised
* ½ cucumber, roughly chopped
* 1 red salad onion or 4 spring onions, sliced
* 1 apple, cored and roughly chopped
* 8 radishes, washed, trimmed and sliced
* 1 tablespoon sunflower seeds
* 1 tablespoon pumpkin seeds
* 120g natural yoghurt
* juice ½ lemon
* 1 tablespoon olive oil
* 1 tablespoon cider vinegar

Mix everything together and serve. Will keep a day or two in the fridge. Great with feta cheese, tinned tuna and/or a hard-boiled egg for extra protein.

COURGETTE SALAD

 & (IF OMITTING THE PARMESAN)

* 1 courgette, spiralised or cut into batons
* 100g fresh or frozen peas
* small handful basil leaves
* 2 tablespoons olive oil
* 2 cloves garlic, peeled
* 1 dessertspoon pine nuts
* 2 tablespoons grated Parmesan
* salt and freshly ground black pepper

Put the courgette and peas in a pan with enough boiling water almost to cover. Cook rapidly for about 3–4 minutes and drain. In a blender, or using a handheld blender, whizz the basil, garlic, olive oil, pine nuts and Parmesan. Season to taste and spoon on to the courgette and peas. Add a further small sprinkle of grated Parmesan and serve immediately.

BLACK BEAN 'GREEK' SALAD

* 1x 400g tin black beans (also called turtle beans), drained and rinsed
* 50g (vegetarian) feta, crumbled
* 4 spring onions, sliced
* 3 tomatoes, roughly chopped
* 6 olives, pitted and roughly chopped
* 4 roasted artichoke hearts in oil from a jar, chopped in half
* small handful basil leaves and a couple sprigs fresh mint, torn
* juice ½ lemon
* 1 teaspoon olive oil
* pepper

Mix everything together and serve at room temperature.

ANOTHER 'GREEK'-STYLE SALAD

* 4 roasted artichoke hearts in oil from a jar, chopped in half
* 6 olives, pitted and roughly chopped
* 1 red onion, finely sliced
* 6 radishes, washed, trimmed and sliced
* ½ cucumber, roughly chopped
* ½ red pepper, deseeded and roughly chopped
* small handful flat-leafed parsley, chopped
* 50g (vegetarian) feta, crumbled
* juice ½ lemon
* 1 teaspoon cider vinegar
* 1 teaspoon olive oil
* freshly ground black pepper

Mix everything together and serve at room temperature. Add rocket, watercress and tomatoes if available.

LOVELY SALAD NUMBER ONE

* 1 little gem lettuce per person
* 1 red onion, sliced
* 1 green pepper, deseeded and sliced
* 1 cucumber, sliced
* 1 clove garlic, crushed
* small handful chopped parsley
* 8 black olives, pitted and roughly chopped
* ½ (vegetarian) Camembert torn into chunks
* 1 tablespoon pumpkin and sunflower seeds
* 1 tablespoon olive oil
* 1 tablespoon vinegar of your choice
* pinch salt and pepper
* juice ½ lemon

Mix everything together in a large salad bowl and serve at once. A few slices of torn salami or parma ham make a smoky addition.

LOVELY SALAD NUMBER TWO

* 200g fresh peas (or frozen peas, thawed)
* 1 green pepper, deseeded and sliced
* ½ cucumber, spiralised or chopped
* 1 fennel bulb, finely sliced
* 1 raw beetroot, spiralised or grated
* 6–8 radishes, washed, trimmed and sliced
* 4 walnuts, chopped into small pieces
* 1 crunchy dessert apple, skin on, roughly chopped
* 1 tablespoon mixed pumpkin and sunflower seeds
* 80g (vegetarian) feta, crumbled

DRESSING:

* 1 tablespoon olive oil
* 1 tablespoon vinegar
* juice ½ lemon
* salt and pepper

Mix all the vegetables, walnuts, apple and mixed seeds in a pretty bowl. Whisk the dressing ingredients, pour over the salad and toss. Crumble the feta on top and serve. If there is any left over, it will keep quite happily until the next day. The apple won't go brown because of the vinegar and lemon juice.

GRIDDLED COURGETTE AND LENTIL SALAD

  (IF OMITTING THE YOGHURT)

* 1 courgette per person
* 1x 250g pouch ready-cooked Puy lentils
* 1 tablespoon olive oil
* 8 cherry tomatoes, cut in half
* 1 stick celery, finely sliced
* 1 small red onion, finely sliced
* whatever fresh herbs you have available, or a mixture of basil, parsley, chives

DRESSING:

* 1 tablespoon natural yoghurt
* ½ tablespoon red wine vinegar
* 1 tablespoon olive oil
* salt and pepper

Using a vegetable peeler cut the courgettes lengthwise into long ribbons, lightly cover them in olive oil and griddle on both sides until they have begun to take on a little colour but still with a bit of crunch. Combine the Puy lentils, cherry tomatoes, cucumber, celery, red onion, basil, parsley and chives and stir in the dressing before laying the courgettes on top.

RAW MIXED VEGETABLE SALAD

  (IF OMITTING EGG)

* ½ cucumber, spiralised or sliced
* 1 medium beetroot, spiralised or chopped
* 1 medium courgette, spiralised or chopped
* 1–2 medium carrots, spiralised or grated
* 1 green pepper, deseeded and chopped finely
* 1 medium fennel bulb, sliced finely
* 1 tablespoon each pumpkin and sunflower seeds
* 1 egg, hard-boiled and sliced
* 1 tablespoon chopped parsley

VINAIGRETTE:

* olive oil
* 1 teaspoon Dijon mustard
* balsamic vinegar
* ⅓ vinegar to ⅔ olive oil put into a jam jar with a teaspoon of Dijon mustard, salt and pepper
* Shake well.

Arrange the different vegetables in patterns on a flat serving dish, top with the egg, chopped parsley and seeds and dress with vinaigrette.

SALAD BOWL MEDLEY

* 1 little gem lettuce
* 100g watercress, thoroughly washed
* 1 raw beetroot, grated or spiralised
* 1 carrot, grated
* ½ cucumber, spiralised, sliced or roughly chopped
* 1 green pepper, deseeded and sliced
* 6 spring onions, sliced
* 1 tablespoon each pumpkin and sunflower seeds
* 1 apple, roughly chopped
* 1 orange, peeled and cut into segments
* 1 tablespoon pea shoots (optional)
* small handful rocket

VINAIGRETTE:

* juice 1 orange
* 1 dessertspoon sherry vinegar
* 1 tablespoon olive oil
* Salt and pepper
* 1 clove garlic, crushed (optional)

Toss all the ingredients together in a vinaigrette made from sherry vinegar, olive or rapeseed oil, salt and pepper plus garlic if you want an extra kick.

It is very easy to grow you own pea shoots and rocket even if you don't own a garden or any outside space. Fill two trays with ordinary compost and scatter the seeds fairly thickly. Leave the rocket seeds (which are very small) as they land and cover with a fine dusting of more compost or vermiculite but push the peas just beneath the surface and cover with a layer of compost. Water and leave in a light place. They should germinate pretty quickly and then you are ready to use them as cut-and-come-again additions to salads.

LATE SUMMER SALAD

* 1 large fresh corn cob, outer husks discarded or 1x 160g tin, drained
* 40g diced pancetta
* 1 fennel bulb, sliced
* ½ cucumber, roughly chopped
* 1 red onion, finely chopped
* handful any fresh herbs you have to hand, finely chopped
* 1 little gem lettuce

VINAIGRETTE:

* juice ½ lemon
* 2 tablespoons olive oil
* salt and pepper
* 1 tablespoon wine or cider vinegar

DO NOT add any salt when boiling the corn – it will toughen the kernels. Drain and run under the cold tap so that it is cool enough to remove the corn with a sharp knife. Heat a small pan and fry the pancetta until crispy. Keep the fat for another time; an egg fried in it is delicious. Wash, shake and tear the lettuce and put into a bowl. Add the fennel, cucumber and herbs then scatter over the corn and pancetta. Dress with the vinaigrette and serve at once.

TIP: to bulk it out, add hard-boiled egg(s), chopped walnuts, pumpkin and sunflower seeds, a tin of tuna or some prawns.

EGG SALAD PLATTER

* 2 hard-boiled eggs
* 200g French beans
* small handful flat-leafed parsley
* 3–4 raw beetroots, the smaller the better
* 200g cherry tomatoes, cut in half
* ½ cucumber, sliced
* small handful fresh basil, roughly torn

DRESSING:

* 2 tablespoons good-quality mayonnaise
* 1 tablespoon crème fraîche
* splash olive oil
* 1 tablespoon red wine vinegar
* salt and pepper
* 1 tablespoon chopped parsley
* 1 teaspoon Dijon mustard (optional)

Rinse the beetroots and tear (not cut or they will 'bleed') the stalks and place in a pan, covering them with cold water. Bring to the boil and simmer until cooked through. With small beets, this shouldn't take too long, maybe 20–30 minutes. Drain and rinse with cold water. When cool enough to handle rub off the skins and trim the ends with a knife, slice and put into a dish. Top and tail the French beans and cook quickly in boiling water, refreshing them under the cold tap. Assemble everything on a pretty dish and pour over the dressing. Serve with some French bread and the beetroot in a separate bowl.

AUTUMN SALAD

* 2 endives, sliced
* 10 mixed radishes, washed, trimmed and sliced
* 1 red onion, finely sliced
* 100g watercress, thoroughly washed
* 1 tablespoon grated Cheddar
* 6 walnuts, broken into small pieces
* 3–4 slices Parma ham, roughly torn
* 1 tablespoon sunflower oil
* 1 tablespoon cider vinegar
* salt and pepper
* 1–2 teaspoons walnut oil (if available)

Mix all the ingredients in a bowl, toss and serve immediately.

POWER-PACKED RAW SALAD

Energy lunch full of goodness and fit for a dull day.

* 200g celeriac, peeled and grated
* 1 raw beetroot, peeled and grated
* 8 radishes, washed, trimmed and sliced
* 1 carrot, grated
* a few chopped chives
* 1 tablespoon each sunflower and pumpkin seeds
* 1 heaped tablespoon mayonnaise
* 1 teaspoon Dijon mustard

Lay all the ingredients into a pretty bowl or dish, mix the mayonnaise and mustard and pour over. Toss to coat everything with the dressing and serve at once.

WINTER SALAD WITH SARDINES

Make up the quantities as needed with:

* radicchio
* beetroot (raw), grated or spiralised
* carrot, grated or spiralised
* radishes, sliced
* spring onions, sliced
* 1x 135g tin sardines (cut each fish in half and remove bones and roe)
* 80g mixed salad leaves with rocket
* sunflower and pumpkin seeds
* 1 green pepper, deseeded and sliced
* 1 lemon

Layer the vegetables on a large platter with the sardines on top and drizzle with your favourite vinaigrette dressing, bottled or freshly made. Serve with a lemon cut into wedges.

VEGETABLES AND SAVOURIES

When I was four years old my father presented my mother with forty point-of-lay chickens, the idea being that we would sell the eggs to Mr Hasler, the village baker. Matters went to plan in spite of a visit from Mr Fox who kidnapped my brothers' and my bantams. Out of the blue, the supply of eggs ceased completely. My parents were mystified, thinking the girls had been traumatised by the rogue intruder. A few days later my mother's radar sensed that the house had become unnaturally quiet and I was nowhere to be seen. She eventually found me behind the tool shed happily stirring a sloppy soup in a galvanised bucket. Then something took Ma's attention and she walked over to the flint wall separating our garden from next door's field and there, in the long grass, lay a pile of empty eggshells. I confessed to having pinched the eggs every day before school in order to put them into a special 'pie'. I saw Ma's mouth twitch and knew, with relief, that I wasn't going to get both barrels. Instead of a severe drubbing she led me into the kitchen and started to teach me how to cook eggs properly – a prime case of egg poacher turned gamekeeper.

I love eggs in all their forms and they are a staple item of my diet, eating one nearly every day of the year, hence the inclusion of this miracle of nature in many of my salads and savoury dishes.

PERFECT POACHED EGG AND BAKED TOMATOES

* 6 cherry tomatoes or two large ones
* salt and freshly ground black pepper
* 1 large organic free-range egg

Preheat the oven to 180°C (fan). Cut the cherry tomatoes in half or slice the large ones and place in a small ovenproof dish. Season and bake for about 10 minutes. Three-quarters fill a small saucepan with water and bring to the boil. If you are not sure quite how fresh your egg is (and the fresher the better) add ½ teaspoon of white wine or cider vinegar to the water. Break the egg into a small dish and check for any shell (remove using one half of the egg shell, which will attract the stray piece) and slide it into the boiling water. There is no need to whisk or stir this beforehand. The fresher the egg, the longer it needs to remain in the boiling water but generally 2–3 minutes is enough. Remove with a slotted spoon and drain on a piece of kitchen paper. Toast a slice of bread if wanted and pile on the tomatoes, topping with the poached egg and cress.

FARMHOUSE EGGS

* 4 hard-boiled eggs, chopped
* 900g potatoes
* 275ml white sauce (see recipe page 175)
* 4 tablespoons grated (vegetarian) cheese
* 50g butter
* salt and pepper

Preheat the oven to 180°C (fan). Boil the potatoes and mash with half the butter. Spread over the bottom of a shallow gratin dish and push up the edge to make a wall. Fold the chopped eggs into the white sauce and pour onto the mashed potato. Sprinkle with the grated cheese and dot with the remaining butter. Bake in the oven until bubbling and golden.

QUAIL EGG NIBBLES

Cook the quail eggs according to the pack instructions and plunge into cold water. Peel and serve with a dish of celery salt. Fiddly but delicious.

EGG AND LENTIL CURRY

* 6 hard-boiled eggs
* 5cm piece fresh ginger, grated
* 1 green chilli, deseeded and finely sliced
* 1 large clove garlic, crushed
* 1 tablespoon curry paste – choose how hot you like it
* 4 cardamom pods, crushed
* 225g dry green lentils, thoroughly washed
* 1x 225g tin coconut milk
* 1 tablespoon concentrated tomato purée
* 275ml water
* 1 teaspoon vegetable oil
* 250g baby spinach
* small handful chopped fresh coriander
* salt and freshly ground black pepper

Fry the ginger, garlic, chilli, curry paste and cardamoms in the vegetable oil for 1–2 minutes. Stir in the lentils, coconut milk, tomato purée and water. Bring to the boil and simmer for 30–40 minutes or until the lentils are cooked. You may need to add a little more water during the cooking. Stir in the spinach and the coriander. Snuggle in the eggs and cook for about 5 minutes or until the eggs are piping hot. Sprinkle with a little more coriander and serve in the cooking dish either on its own or with plain basmati rice and mango chutney.

POACHED EGG WITH CRUSHED AVOCADO, RED ONION, TOMATOES AND CORIANDER

Bitterly cold day. Breakfast was a perfectly poached egg on top of crushed avocado mixed with finely chopped red onion, cherry tomatoes, coriander, lime juice and salt and pepper.

CHEAT'S TOMATOES A LA PROVENCALE

* 1 large beef tomato per person, cut in half
* 1 packet luxury bread sauce
* 2 tablespoons chopped parsley
* 1 clove garlic, crushed
* salt and pepper
* 1–1 ½ tablespoons olive oil

Preheat the oven to 180˚C (fan). Place the halved tomatoes cut side up in an ovenproof dish. In a bowl, mix the packet of bread sauce with the parsley and garlic and spoon on to the tomatoes. Season with a little salt and lots of pepper, drizzle with olive oil and bake for about 15–20 minutes. This makes a great side dish to lamb chops or simply on its own popped on slices of toast or fried bread.

BAKED MARROW

* 1kg marrow, cut in 5cm slices and seeds removed
* 6–8 cherry tomatoes, halved
* cheese sauce (recipe page 76)
* 1 tablespoon panko crumbs

Preheat oven to 180˚C (fan). Place the marrow slices in an ovenproof dish and cover with the cheese sauce. Scatter the cherry tomatoes and sprinkle with the panko crumbs. Bake for about 20 minutes until bubbling and brown.

BAKED SWISS CHARD WITH AN EGG

(V) (GF)

* 150g Swiss chard leaves
* 1 egg
* 2 tablespoons crème fraîche
* 75g (vegetarian) grated cheese
* 8 cherry tomatoes, cut in half
* salt and pepper

Preheat oven to 180°C (fan). Blanch the chard in a little boiling water for 3 minutes. Drain well, roughly chop and place in an ovenproof dish. Mix the crème fraîche, cheese and tomatoes and season with salt and pepper. Pour over the chard and bake for about 10 minutes. Remove from the oven, make a well in the centre and drop in an egg. Bake a further 5 minutes or until the white is set and the yolk still runny.

BAKED CHARD AND COURGETTES

(GF)

* 200g Swiss chard
* 1 red onion, sliced
* 2 courgettes, sliced
* 1 clove garlic, chopped
* 2–3 heaped tablespoons grated Gruyère cheese (or Cheddar)
* 100g smoked pancetta, diced
* salt and pepper
* olive oil

Preheat the oven to 180°C (fan). Slice the chard and put in a pan with enough boiling water just to cover. Stir and cook for 3–4 minutes. Drain well. Fry the pancetta until crisp and put to one side. In the same pan fry the onion in the pancetta fat until soft. Add the garlic then mix everything together before tipping into a shallow gratin dish. Sprinkle over the grated cheese and drizzle with the olive oil. Bake for about 20 minutes or until bubbling and golden.

INDIAN CARROTS

* As many carrots as you need, peeled and sliced diagonally, 2 per person
* 1 tablespoon cardamom pods
* butter
* ½ teaspoon sugar
* salt
* water – enough barely to cover the carrots

Put the sliced carrots into a pan with the cardamom, butter, sugar, salt and water. Cover with a lid and bring to the boil for 5 minutes. Remove the lid, reduce the heat and simmer until the water has evaporated, the carrots are cooked and glazed with the juices. If you have time, pick out the cardamom pods before serving.

CARROTS WITH SPRING ONIONS

* 2 carrots per person, sliced diagonally
* 6 spring onions, sliced
* 1 dessertspoon butter
* ½ teaspoon sugar
* pinch salt
* 1 tablespoon freshly chopped parsley

Melt the butter in a shallow pan and add the vegetables along with the sugar, salt and enough water barely to cover the carrots. Bring to the boil, reduce the heat and simmer for about ¼ hour or until most of the water has evaporated. Sprinkle with the chopped parsley and serve.

GREEN VEGETABLE BAKE WITH BUTTER BEANS

* 1x 400g tin butter beans, drained and rinsed
* 1 leek, sliced
* 200g Swiss chard or 200g baby spinach
* 100g kale
* cheese sauce (see page 76)

Preheat the oven to 180°C (fan). Slice the leek and put in a large pan with the chard leaves or baby spinach. Pour on a little boiling water and cook for 5 minutes. Drain well and tip into an ovenproof dish. Add the butter beans and pour over the cheese sauce. Bake for about 20 minutes until bubbling and golden.

CARROT AND PARSNIP GRATIN

* 300g parsnips, peeled and grated
* 450g carrots, grated
* 25g butter
* 2 banana shallots, sliced
* 150ml double cream or 150ml crème fraîche
* salt and pepper
* freshly grated nutmeg

Preheat the oven to 180°C (fan). Blanch the carrots and parsnips in a saucepan with boiling water for 2 minutes. Drain well. Melt the butter in a frying pan and cook the shallots until they become transparent but not brown. Tip into a gratin dish and add the parsnips and carrots. Season with salt and pepper and pour over the crème fraîche/double cream. Mix well and grate a pinch of nutmeg on top. Cover loosely with aluminium foil and bake for approximately 1 hour or until soft. Perfect with roast beef.

VEGETABLE FRITTATA

* 1 courgette, roughly chopped
* 1 red onion, chopped
* 1 stick celery, sliced
* 1x 160g tin unsweetened corn, drained
* handful basil or fresh coriander, roughly chopped
* 1 egg, beaten
* pinch dried chilli flakes or 1 fresh red chilli, deseeded and finely sliced
* 1 teaspoon paprika
* 1 tablespoon gram flour
* oil
* salt and pepper

Mix everything but the oil together. Heat a tablespoon of oil in a non-stick pan and pour in the vegetables. Cook on a medium heat for about 5 minutes then put a plate on top and turn the pan upside down so the frittata lands on the plate. Put the pan back on the heat and slide in the frittata to cook the other side for a further 5 minutes. Serve with a simple green salad.

MIXED VEGETABLE BAKE

This can be prepared in advance and heated up later.

* 1 courgette, sliced
* 3 tomatoes, sliced
* 2 red onions, sliced
* 3 new potatoes in their skins, scrubbed and sliced
* 1 clove garlic, chopped
* 3 tablespoons olive oil
* handful fresh basil
* 2 teaspoons dried oregano
* salt and pepper
* 77g pancetta, diced
* 2 tablespoons fresh brown breadcrumbs
* 1 tablespoon grated cheese of your choice

FOR THE CHEESE SAUCE:

* 1 tablespoon butter
* 1 tablespoon flour
* 275ml milk
* 2 tablespoons grated cheese of your choice
* 1 teaspoon Dijon mustard
* 150ml crème fraîche
* salt and pepper

Preheat the grill on high. Put all the prepared vegetables into a baking dish, add the garlic, drizzle with olive oil and sprinkle with the herbs. Season with salt and pepper and bake on the middle shelf until the vegetables are beginning to soften and brown, but not burned. You may need to cover them loosely with a piece of foil. Put the pancetta into a pan and fry until crisp. Remove and keep warm. Make the cheese sauce: melt the butter with the flour and cook for 2 minutes, stirring all the while. Whisk in the milk to prevent lumps from forming and bring to the boil. Once thickened, remove from the heat and add the cheese and mustard, then the crème fraîche and season with salt and pepper. Pour the cheese sauce over the cooked vegetables, scatter the pancetta on top. Mix the breadcrumbs with any remaining grated cheese and sprinkle over the dish before putting under the grill until bubbling and brown.

PARSNIP AND PETITS POIS FRITTERS

  (IF USING GRAIN CHICKPEA FLOUR)

* 300g parsnips, peeled and chopped into small chunks
* 200g frozen petits pois
* 4 spring onions, sliced
* 150g baby spinach
* 1 teaspoon medium curry powder
* 150g grated cheese (Cheddar, Gruyère, etc.)
* 1 level tablespoon wholemeal flour
* 1 egg, beaten
* handful coriander, roughly chopped
* salt and pepper

Boil the parsnips until soft. While the parsnips are cooking steam the baby spinach above for a couple of minutes to wilt it. Drain the parsnips and mash them and allow to cool before incorporating all the other ingredients. Heat a tablespoon of oil in a non-stick pan and drop in spoonfuls of the mixture, turning once after 2–3 minutes. Serve piping hot with mango chutney.

GRATIN WITH POTATO AND FENNEL

* 2–3 medium-sized potatoes, peeled and finely sliced
* 1 fennel bulb, sliced
* 275ml full-fat milk
* 150g (vegetarian) grated cheese
* salt and pepper

Preheat the oven to 180°C (fan). Put the potatoes and fennel in a pan with the milk, bring to the boil and simmer gently for about 6 minutes. Season with salt and pepper and pour into a buttered ovenproof dish and top with the grated cheese. Bake for about 20 minutes or until bubbling and brown.

PETITS POIS A LA FRANCAISE

This is an ideal vegetable dish to prepare in advance and it reheats well. It goes with meat or poultry.

* 500g frozen petits pois
* 6 spring onions, sliced
* 2 hearty little gem lettuces, cut into quarters
* 1 tablespoon butter
* ½ teaspoon sugar
* salt to taste

Melt the butter in a saucepan and add the petits pois, spring onions and lettuce. Stir in the sugar and salt adding a little water – about 3 tablespoons. Bring to the boil, reduce the heat and simmer for about ¼ hour, stirring every now and again, checking that there is enough liquid to prevent burning.

OMELETTE WITH SPRING ONIONS, PARSLEY, ASPARAGUS AND A HINT OF GRATED PARMESAN

* 2 organic free-range eggs
* 100g asparagus tips, sliced
* 3 spring onions, sliced
* 1 tablespoon grated Parmesan
* butter or vegetable oil
* salt and freshly ground black pepper

Begin by steaming or boiling the asparagus for a couple of minutes then drain. Whisk the eggs and season with salt and freshly ground black pepper. Heat a non-stick frying/omelette-sized pan and add the butter or oil. Heat but don't allow to smoke and pour in the eggs. Swizzle with a fork or with a spatula a couple of times before adding the asparagus and spring onions. Sprinkle over the Parmesan. Tip the pan so that any remaining runny egg is cooked, flip over and serve immediately.

LITTLE GREEN CABBAGE BUNDLES

This is a good way to make a small cabbage go further.

* 250g Savoy cabbage
* butter
* juice ½ lemon
* salt and pepper

First, remove any damaged leaves and discard. Then cut off six more leaves, cutting away the rib but keeping each leaf whole. Place in a pan of boiling water and cook for a minute to blanch them. Drain and place in a bowl of cold water. Cut the remaining cabbage in half and remove the core before slicing very thinly. Take out the blanched cabbage leaves and fill each with some of the sliced raw cabbage. Dot with butter, a little lemon juice and salt and pepper. Carefully fold each leaf to make little bundles, tucking them underneath. Place on the bottom of a steamer and cook for about 8–10 minutes.

MANGETOUT, LEEK AND LETTUCE STEW

* 160g mangetout
* 1 leek, sliced
* 1 little gem lettuce, sliced
* 1 tablespoon olive oil
* pinch salt
* pinch sugar

Put everything into a wok on a high heat for 2 minutes then reduce the heat, cover and simmer for about 6–8 minutes, stirring every now and again, checking that there is sufficient moisture to prevent burning. This can be prepared in advance and reheated and served alongside fish, chicken, any other meat or pasta.

LENTIL AND VEGETABLE BAKE

* 100g dried yellow lentils
* 1 aubergine (250g), sliced
* 1 red onion, sliced
* 1 carrot, finely chopped
* 1 stick celery, sliced
* 1x 400g tin cherry tomatoes
* 1 vegetable stock pot
* 500 ml water
* ½ red chilli, deseeded and sliced
* ½ teaspoon dried mixed herbs
* 2 cloves garlic, chopped
* salt and pepper

FOR THE TOPPING:

* 150g swede, peeled and roughly chopped
* 1 large red sweet potato (250g), peeled and roughly chopped

Preheat the oven to 180°C (fan). Mix the vegetable stock pot with the water in a saucepan and add the lentils. Bring to the boil and cook for 10 minutes on a good rolling boil, reduce the heat, cover and simmer according to the pack instructions. Use a low-calorie olive oil spray (about four squirts) to coat a wide, shallow pan or wok. Add the carrot, onion and celery and sweat for about 3 minutes before adding the garlic, tomatoes and lentils and herbs along with any remaining cooking liquid. Stir, cover and cook for about 5 minutes to bring up to the boil. Add the aubergine slices, stir, cover again and simmer until all the vegetables are cooked. Cover the swede and sweet potato with cold water, bring to the boil, cover and cook until soft. Add a little olive oil or butter if wished. Mash and season with salt and pepper. Tip the vegetable mixture into a shallow gratin dish and cover with the mashed swede and sweet potato, spreading it with a fork. Either bake immediately until it is bubbling or keep to one side for later.

STUFFED CABBAGE LEAVES WITH RED SAUCE

For 2 as a light meal or starter

* Several outer leaves cabbage, lower thick rib removed
* 1x 400g tin green lentils, drained and rinsed
* 50g (vegetarian) feta, crumbled
* 1 carrot, grated
* 1 red onion, finely chopped
* 1 large clove garlic, crushed
* 1 heaped teaspoon capers
* salt and pepper
* olive oil

Blanch the cabbage leaves in a little boiling water for a minute or two, drain and allow to cool. In a small pan, heat a teaspoon of olive oil and gently sweat the onion, carrot and garlic for a couple of minutes. In a separate bowl, mix the lentils, carrot mixture, capers and feta. Overlap the cabbage leaves (or use a single one if large enough) and pile on half the mixture. Carefully fold over the leaves to make a little bundle, tucking the edges in, and place in a steamer. Cook for about 15 minutes and serve with the red sauce.

FOR THE RED SAUCE:

* ½ red pepper, deseeded and roughly chopped
* 6 cherry tomatoes, roughly chopped
* 1 stick celery, sliced
* 1 clove garlic, crushed
* 1 teaspoon concentrated tomato purée
* 1 tablespoon olive oil
* salt and pepper
* a little water or vegetable stock

Put everything into a small pan with enough liquid just to cover, bring to the boil and simmer gently until the liquid has evaporated and the sauce has thickened. Whizz with a handheld blender, check for seasoning and serve hot with the cabbage parcels.

HOMEMADE HUMMUS

* 1 tablespoon tahini paste
* 1x 400g tin chickpeas, drained and rinsed
* 1 clove garlic, roughly chopped
* 1 tablespoon olive oil
* juice ½ lemon
* water as necessary
* smoked paprika

Put all the ingredients into a blender and whizz, adding enough cold water to slacken it so that it isn't too stiff nor runny but will hold its shape on a plate. Put into a pretty bowl and drizzle over a little extra olive oil and a dusting of paprika. Serve with crisp bread and crudités such as sticks of cucumber, celery, carrot and sweet peppers.

SWEETCORN AND KALE FRITTER

* 1 fresh corn cob, outer husks removed and discarded or 1x 160g tin, drained
* 150g bowl kale, stripped from the stalks and roughly chopped
* 1 teaspoon crunchy peanut butter
* 1 egg
* 1–2 teaspoons gram flour
* handful fresh coriander, roughly chopped
* 1 green chilli, deseeded and finely chopped
* 2 spring onions, sliced
* low-fat olive oil cooking spray
* salt and pepper

Strip the corn from the cob and blanch in boiling water with the kale for about a minute. Drain thoroughly and allow to cool slightly. In a bowl, whisk the egg with the gram flour, chilli, spring onions, coriander, salt and pepper and the peanut butter. Stir in the corn and kale. Spray a small non-stick pan with a little low-fat oil and tip in the mixture. Allow to cook on a moderate heat for about 5 minutes before flipping on to a plate. Add another couple of sprays of oil to the pan and slide in the fritter to cook the other side for a further 2 minutes. Serve at once with some sort of salad.

SWEETCORN PATTY

* 1 fresh corn cob, outer husks removed and discarded
* 1 egg
* 1 heaped teaspoon gram flour
* handful fresh coriander, roughly chopped
* salt and freshly ground black pepper
* 1 tablespoon grated Parmesan
* 3 spring onions, trimmed and finely sliced
* vegetable oil

Strip the corn kernels and blanch in a little boiling water for a minute, drain and allow to cool slightly. In a small bowl, beat the egg with the gram flour, Parmesan, salt and freshly ground black pepper. Fold in the corn, spring onions and coriander. Heat a teaspoon of vegetable oil in a small, non-stick frying pan and tip in the corn batter. Spread and allow to cook on a medium heat for about 3 minutes. Take a clean plate, place over the pan and empty the corn patty onto the plate. Place the pan back on a medium heat and slide in the patty to cook on the other side for a further 2–3 minutes. Serve at once with a green salad and some mango chutney or hot chilli jelly.

HEALTHY CORN SALAD

* 1x 160g tin sweetcorn, drained
* 1 red and 1 green pepper, deseeded and roughly chopped
* 1 small red onion, finely sliced
* 1 small apple, roughly chopped
* ⅓ cucumber, roughly chopped
* handful black pitted olives, roughly chopped
* 1 tablespoon each of pumpkin and sunflower seeds
* 6 cherry tomatoes, quartered
* small handful basil leaves, roughly torn at the last moment
* 1 tablespoon cider vinegar
* 1 tablespoon olive oil
* salt and pepper

Mix all the vegetables in a large bowl, then separately whisk the vinegar, olive oil, salt and pepper before incorporating into the salad ingredients. Add the torn basil leaves and mix well.

SWEETCORN AND KIDNEY BEAN SALAD

* 1x 160g tin sweetcorn, salt- and sugar-free
* 1x 400g tin kidney beans, drained and rinsed
* 1 stick celery, sliced
* 1 red onion, sliced
* 1 red and 1 yellow pepper, deseeded and roughly chopped
* 50g walnuts, roughly chopped
* juice ½ lemon
* dash olive oil
* salt and pepper
* a few basil leaves

Mix everything together and scatter with basil leaves. Keeps well for the next day.

BITSA THIS, BITSA THAT... VEGETABLE FLAN

* 1 courgette, roughly chopped
* ½ green pepper, roughly chopped
* 1 leek, sliced
* 100g chestnut mushrooms, roughly chopped or sliced
* 2 tomatoes, roughly chopped
* 150g florets cauliflower, roughly chopped or sliced
* 30g basil
* 30g parsley
* 3 tablespoons olive oil
* crème fraîche
* 1 tablespoon grated Parmesan
* ¼ teaspoon grated nutmeg
* 1 egg
* 1 tablespoon gram flour
* 1 teaspoon Dijon mustard
* salt and pepper

Preheat the oven to 180°C (fan). Put the vegetables into a shallow gratin dish and drizzle over a little olive oil. Season lightly and cover with foil. Bake for about 20 minutes until soft and nearly cooked through. Beat the egg with the crème fraîche, the gram flour, Parmesan and mustard. Stir in the herbs and season lightly. Pour over the vegetables and bake a further 8–10 minutes until bubbling.

BAKED AUBERGINE

  & (IF OMITTING THE PARMESAN) GF

* 1 aubergine (250g)
* 1 red onion, sliced
* 6 tomatoes, roughly chopped
* 1 large clove garlic, crushed
* 30g mixed fresh herbs: parsley, basil, oregano or 1 teaspoon mixed dried herbs
* olive oil
* 1 tablespoon concentrated tomato purée
* 2 tablespoons grated Parmesan
* 1 tablespoon mixed seeds: pumpkin, sesame and sunflower
* salt and freshly ground black pepper

Preheat the oven to 180°C (fan). Cut the aubergine in half lengthways, scoop out most of the flesh with a spoon, but leaving enough to keep the shells firm; place them in a shallow ovenproof dish. Heat a teaspoon of olive oil in a wok, add the onion and stir for a minute then moisten with some water. Leave to cook on a medium heat, stirring every now and again, for about 5 minutes or until the water has evaporated but the onion is soft. Roughly chop the aubergine flesh and add to the onion along with the tomatoes, garlic, tomato purée and herbs. Season well with salt and freshly ground black pepper and cook for about 2 minutes before piling into the empty aubergine shells. Spoon on the mixed seeds, top with the Parmesan and finish with a further drizzle of olive oil. Pour a little water into the pan around the aubergines and bake for about 30–40 minutes or until they are thoroughly cooked and bubbling. Either eat straight away or cool and refrigerate to reheat the next day.

CHARGRILLED ASPARAGUS WITH CRUNCHY PEANUT BUTTER

V VG DF GF

* 110g asparagus
* 1 heaped teaspoon crunchy peanut butter
* olive oil
* juice ½ lemon
* 2 teaspoons balsamic vinegar
* salt and freshly ground black pepper

Trim and blanch the asparagus in a little boiling water for about 2 minutes. Drain, cool slightly and put in a shallow dish. Sprinkle with a little olive oil. Slacken the peanut butter with the lemon juice and gently rub as much of the paste as you can onto the asparagus spears. Heat a griddle pan and when hot but not smoking, add the asparagus, turning every now and again. Cook for about 2 minutes and remove. Mix the salad ingredients with the balsamic vinegar and a splash more olive oil and serve with the asparagus placed on top.

MIXED CHERRY TOMATO AND ASPARAGUS BAKE

* 300g mixed cherry tomatoes, halved, enough to cover the bottom of a shallow ovenproof dish
* 125g asparagus spears, trimmed and cut into 3cm pieces
* 1 free-range egg
* 1 tablespoon gram flour
* 150g cream cheese
* 3 tablespoons crème fraîche
* 2–3 tablespoons grated Parmesan
* 1 tablespoon each chives and basil, roughly chopped
* salt and freshly ground black pepper

Preheat the oven to 180°C (fan). Lightly steam the asparagus for about 3 minutes, drain and leave to cool. Lay the halved tomatoes in the bottom of the dish and scatter over the asparagus. In a small bowl beat the egg with the gram flour and add the other ingredients, mixing well. Spread over the vegetables and bake for about 30 minutes until bubbling.

ASPARAGUS, SPRING ONION, HERB AND CHEESE BAKE

* 125g asparagus, enough to cover the bottom of your ovenproof dish, sliced
* 4 spring onions, sliced
* 4 eggs
* 1 heaped tablespoon gram flour
* 1 tablespoon milk
* 150ml crème fraîche
* 3–4 tablespoons cheese: I use whatever I have in the fridge. This one was a mixture of Parmesan, Cheddar and crumbled feta
* salt and pepper
* 1 tablespoon mixed herbs: parsley and chives for example

Preheat the oven to 180°C (fan). Whisk the eggs into the gram flour one by one making sure there are no lumps. Then whisk in the milk, crème fraîche, cheese and salt and pepper. Lay the asparagus, spring onions and chopped herbs on the bottom of your ovenproof dish, pour over the custard and bake until golden brown and fluffed up. Serve at room temperature with a salad of your choice.

POACHED EGG AND BABY SPINACH

 (IF OMITTING RYVITA)

* 1 very fresh egg
* 125g baby spinach leaves

Bring some water up to the boil in a milk pan and drop in the egg; there is no need for any vinegar nor is it necessary to swirl the water first. Wash the spinach and put in a small pan, stirring to reduce the leaves; cook quickly in their own moisture for about 2 minutes. Using a wooden spoon squeeze out as much residual moisture as possible and put onto a plate. After about 2–3 minutes, lift the poached egg with a slotted spoon and drain on some kitchen paper before placing on top of the spinach. Season and serve at once with some dark rye Ryvita.

EGG CURRY (2)

* 2 hard-boiled eggs, kept whole
* 1 red onion, finely chopped
* ½ red chilli, deseeded and finely chopped
* 5cm piece root ginger, peeled and grated
* ½ teaspoon ground turmeric
* 1 tablespoon concentrated tomato purée
* 3 tomatoes, roughly chopped
* ½ teaspoon mustard seeds
* 1 tablespoon vegetable or sunflower oil
* handful fresh coriander leaves, roughly chopped
* salt and freshly ground black pepper
* 1x 400g tin green lentils
* 1 tablespoon sultanas (optional)

In a wok, heat the oil and add the mustard seeds, which will start popping. Immediately add the onion. Stir constantly to prevent burning for 3 minutes then add the root ginger and chilli. Cook for 5 minutes stirring all the while then add the chopped tomatoes, tomato purée, turmeric, sultanas if using and a cupful of water. Bring to the boil and stir in the salt and freshly ground black pepper to taste. Reduce the heat to a gentle simmer, cover and cook for a further 15 minutes or so, making sure there is sufficient liquid, topping up if necessary with a little more water. Place the hard-boiled eggs in the wok with the sauce and reheat them gently. When piping hot, scatter over the coriander leaves and serve with the lentils, a sweet mango chutney and side dishes of cucumber raita, chopped tomatoes and red onion relish and more coriander (see below).

CUCUMBER RAITA

Mix the following together:

* 5cm piece cucumber, grated
* 2 tablespoons natural yoghurt
* pinch salt and freshly ground black pepper
* pinch ground coriander
* 1 heaped teaspoon finely chopped mint

TOMATO AND RED ONION RELISH

Mix the following together:

* 1 tomato, finely chopped
* 1 small red onion, finely chopped
* 1 teaspoon finely chopped fresh coriander leaves

SPAGHETTI WITH BABY VEG STEW

   (IF OMITTING THE PARMESAN)

* 100g dried pasta – I used spaghetti
* 250g baby spinach, chard, mangetout, kale, asparagus, mixture cherry tomatoes
* 1 clove garlic, crushed
* grated Parmesan and Greek basil leaves to sprinkle
* 1 teaspoon virgin olive oil
* salt and freshly ground black pepper

Cook the pasta according to the pack instructions. Heat the oil in a wok and add all the vegetables including the garlic. Stir, cover and cook gently, stirring frequently to prevent burning. You may need to add a splash of water. Season and serve on top of the pasta with the Parmesan and basil.

SPRING VEGETABLE FRITTATA

* 2 free-range eggs
* 1 tablespoon crème fraîche
* 1 tablespoon grated Parmesan
* mixture of young vegetables; baby broad beans, mangetout, asparagus tips
* handful flat-leafed parsley, roughly chopped
* 1 small clove garlic, crushed
* salt and freshly ground black pepper
* 1 teaspoon butter

Turn on your grill to maximum. Cut the mangetout into 2 or 3 pieces, the same with the asparagus, and put in a pan with the broad beans and a little boiling water. Cook for 3 minutes, drain and rinse under the cold tap. Beat the eggs in a bowl with the crème fraîche, Parmesan, parsley, garlic and seasoning. Heat a small non-stick omelette pan and add the butter. When it has melted and is just beginning to turn hazelnut-coloured, pour the egg mixture into the hot pan, turn down the heat to medium and allow to cook gently without stirring for about 5 minutes. Remove from the stove and place under the grill to cook the top for a further 3 minutes or until it is golden brown and firm. Have ready a large plate and put it on top of the pan, turn it upside down and serve at room temperature with a green salad.

HUMMUS WITH CHILLI AND SMOKED PAPRIKA

* 1x 400g tin chickpeas, drained and rinsed
* 1 tablespoon tahini
* juice ½ lemon
* pinch smoked paprika
* ½ chilli of your choice, deseeded and roughly chopped
* 1 tablespoon olive oil
* 1 clove garlic, roughly chopped
* salt
* water

Place everything except the salt and water in a small blender and whiz until smooth. Taste and season accordingly, adding a little water to slacken. Serve in a pretty bowl with a drizzle of extra olive oil and a further sprinkle of paprika.

CHERRY TOMATO AND BABY BROAD BEAN CLAFOUTIS

* 200g or enough cherry tomatoes to cover the bottom of an ovenproof flan dish
* 100g podded baby broad beans or frozen (or other vegetables such as asparagus tips, sliced)
* 200g (vegetarian) Brie, roughly torn
* 4 free-range, organic eggs
* 1 tablespoon gram flour
* 4 tablespoons crème fraîche
* 1 tablespoon milk
* handful flat-leafed parsley, roughly chopped
* handful basil, roughly chopped
* 1 tablespoon grated Parmesan
* 1 slice brown bread made into crumbs (I used a slice of Vogel's soya and linseed bread)
* salt and freshly ground black pepper

Preheat the oven to 180°C (fan). Scatter the tomatoes (cut in half if slightly larger than a cherry) over the bottom of a buttered flan dish, then add the broad beans, Brie and herbs. Beat the eggs with the crème fraîche and add the Parmesan, gram flour, milk and salt and freshly ground black pepper. Pour over the vegetables. Scatter the top with the brown breadcrumbs and a further little grating of Parmesan. Bake for about 30–40 minutes until puffed up and golden brown. Serve at room temperature with a green salad.

SOUFFLE OMELETTE WITH BABY CHARD AND PARMESAN

  (IF OMITTING THE PARMESAN)

* 1 free-range organic egg
* 75g chard (or 110g baby spinach)
* 1 tablespoon grated Parmesan
* salt and freshly ground black pepper
* spray of oil or a hazelnut-sized piece butter

Turn on the grill to full heat. Cook the chard/spinach in a pan with a very little water for 5 minutes, then drain thoroughly and chop. Separate the egg and whisk the white until it is a frothy foam but not stiff. Fold the egg yolk, chard and Parmesan into the whisked white. Heat a small non-stick omelette or frying pan and add the oil/butter, then spoon in the egg mixture. Do not stir or swizzle but allow the base to cook and brown slightly – for about 2 minutes. Place the pan under the hot grill for a further minute or two until puffed up and set. Tip out onto a plate, folding in half, and serve immediately.

AUBERGINE DIP

* 1 aubergine (250g)
* 1 clove garlic, crushed
* 1 tablespoon tahini
* 1 chilli, deseeded and roughly chopped
* juice 1 lemon
* sea salt
* fresh herbs: coriander, parsley, chives
* olive oil

Preheat the oven to 180°C (fan). Slice the aubergine 1cm thick, place on a flat baking tray and very lightly drizzle the olive oil. Sprinkle with a little sea salt and roast in the oven for about 15 minutes or until soft and slightly brown, turning the slices once. Remove from the tray and allow to cool. Put the lemon juice, tahini, chilli and aubergine in a small blender. Add about a tablespoon more of olive oil and blitz, pulsing to make sure everything is blended. Add the herbs and blitz again on pulse. Taste and season if necessary. Serve with a mixture of carrots, peppers and cucumber and/or some wholegrain crisp bread.

SPROUTS, SUGAR SNAP PEAS AND SPINACH

* 200g Brussels sprouts, topped and tailed, sliced or halved
* 160g sugar snap peas, sliced (or mangetout or frozen petits pois)
* 250g baby spinach, thoroughly washed
* 2 tablespoons double cream
* freshly ground nutmeg
* 6 fresh mint leaves, chopped
* salt and pepper

Cook the sprouts and peas in a pan with a little water, covered with a lid, for 3 minutes. Add the spinach, stir and cook a further minute or two. Drain, return to the pan and stir in the double cream, nutmeg, seasoning and the mint leaves.

ASPARAGUS, BROAD BEAN, CHILLI AND JERSEY ROYAL FRITTATA

* 6 eggs (2 hard-boiled)
* 250g asparagus, sliced
* 175g Jersey royal potatoes
* 500g broad beans in their pods (or 250g frozen beans)
* 1 tablespoon parsley, chopped
* ½ red chilli, deseeded and finely chopped
* 1 red onion, finely chopped
* little grated (vegetarian) cheese (optional)
* olive oil
* salt and pepper

Hard-boil two of the eggs, allow to cool then peel and slice. Scrub the potatoes and cut into small chunks before cooking in boiling water until soft. Beat the other eggs in a bowl and add the parsley and cheese and season well. Boil the asparagus and broad beans together for 5 minutes and drain. Heat the grill on high. In a medium-sized non-stick frying pan heat a tablespoon of olive oil and add the onion and chilli. Stir for a couple of minutes then add the asparagus, beans and potatoes. Stir for 5 minutes and then pour on the beaten egg mixture. Do not stir but cook for about 3 minutes before laying the sliced hard-boiled eggs on top. Place the pan under the hot grill for a minute or more until it puffs up and is thoroughly cooked. Place a large plate on top of the pan and carefully upend the frittata on to the plate. Eat at room temperature with a salad. Great cold for picnics or lunch boxes.

MUSHROOM BAKE

* 250g mushrooms of your choice, cleaned and sliced
* 1 tablespoon butter
* 110ml double cream
* 2 tablespoons parsley, chopped
* 2 cloves garlic, chopped
* salt and pepper
* paprika

Preheat the oven to 180°C (fan). Lay the mushroom slices on the bottom of a shallow ovenproof dish. Melt the butter in a small pan with the garlic, cream and parsley. Mix, season well with salt and pepper and pour over the mushrooms. Bake until bubbling and dust with a little paprika before serving.

PEA, BEAN, POTATO AND HERB FRITTATA

* 200g peas, fresh or frozen
* 220g French beans, sliced
* 1 red salad onion, finely sliced
* 175g new potatoes, chopped into small chunks
* 3 eggs
* 2 tablespoons crème fraîche
* 2 tablespoons grated Parmesan
* several sprigs flat-leafed parsley, roughly chopped
* several mint leaves, roughly chopped
* splash oil
* salt and freshly ground black pepper

Put the potatoes on to boil and when nearly cooked (about 6 minutes) add the peas and beans. Cook for a further 5 minutes and remove from heat and drain. Heat a little oil in a medium-sized non-stick frying pan and add the chopped onion. Allow to soften on a gentle heat for about 3 minutes. Turn the grill on full. In a small bowl, beat the eggs with the crème fraîche, add the Parmesan and seasoning. Fold in the herbs. Add the vegetables to the onion in the frying pan, stir and then tip in the egg mixture. Swizzle briefly and leave to cook on a medium/high heat for about 5 minutes. Place the frying pan under the grill and allow to puff up and brown. Place a plate over the pan and tip out the frittata. Allow to cool to room temperature before serving.

COURGETTE AND MOZZARELLA BAKE

 (IF OMITTING THE PANKO/BREADCRUMBS)

* 2 courgettes, sliced
* 4 tomatoes, roughly chopped
* 1x 150g ball fresh mozzarella
* 10 basil leaves
* 2 tablespoons grated Cheddar
* salt and pepper
* 1 tablespoon olive oil
* 1 generous tablespoon panko crumbs or fresh brown breadcrumbs

Preheat the oven to 180°C (fan). Place the courgettes onto a shallow dish and dot with the tomatoes. Tear the mozzarella into small pieces and scatter on top, plus torn basil leaves and grated Cheddar. Season well and top with a good sprinkle of panko breadcrumbs or fresh brown breadcrumbs. Drizzle with olive oil and season well and bake till bubbling and golden.

ROMANO PEPPERS STUFFED WITH SPINACH, TOMATOES, PINE NUTS AND CAPERS

  (IF OMITTING THE PARMESAN)

* 2 Romano peppers
* 1 tablespoon pine nuts
* 1 tablespoon capers, roughly chopped
* 1 chilli of your choice, deseeded and finely chopped
* 1 heaped tablespoon grated Parmesan
* 1 heaped tablespoon curly parsley, roughly chopped
* 1 clove garlic, crushed
* 250g baby spinach
* 1 slice multi-grain bread (or wholemeal) in crumbs
* olive oil
* pepper

Preheat the oven to 180˚C (fan). Cut the peppers in half lengthways and remove the seeds. Place cut side up in a shallow ovenproof dish and drizzle with olive oil. Bake for 15 minutes and remove. Wilt the baby spinach in a saucepan for 2 minutes, run under the cold tap and squeeze out the moisture. In a bowl, mix the pine nuts, capers, parsley, breadcrumbs, Parmesan, garlic and spinach and season with freshly ground black pepper – you shouldn't need any extra salt because of the Parmesan and capers. Spoon the mixture on to the peppers, drizzle with a little more olive oil and bake a further 20–30 minutes or until bubbling and brown. Serve at room temperature with a salad.

CRUSHED AVOCADO ON TOAST WITH CHILLI AND CORIANDER

* 1 ripe avocado, peeled and roughly crushed with a fork
* juice ½ lime
* 1 teaspoon coriander, roughly chopped
* ½ mild chilli, deseeded and finely chopped
* 1 clove garlic, crushed
* 1 slice wholemeal/rye/sourdough/multi-grain bread, toasted
* salt and freshly ground black pepper
* 1 tomato, sliced

Mix the avocado, lime juice, coriander and chilli and season lightly with salt and freshly ground black pepper. Rub the clove of garlic over the toasted bread and pile on the avocado. Decorate with slices of chilli and tomato.

COURGETTE BAKE

Ⓥ

This recipe was given to me by an old friend who told me the following story when the family was employed in the Diplomatic Service in South America. The kitchen was a good distance from the dining room and by the time the food arrived it was no longer hot. There happened to be a serving hatch with direct access to the kitchen and when the next engagement was in the diary she asked the staff to use this. However, disaster struck. On being summoned for the first course, the doors to the hatch opened and then a pair of arms appeared holding a dish, followed by a head and then the entire body before landing on the dining room floor. Oh, the joys of being lost in translation...

* 4–5 courgettes, grated
* 1 large onion, grated
* 60g parsley, chopped
* 3 tablespoons plain flour
* 2 eggs, beaten lightly
* 275g strong grated (vegetarian) cheese
* 2 large tomatoes, sliced
* 1 tablespoon butter
* 1 teaspoon paprika
* salt and pepper

Preheat the oven to 180°C (fan). Mix together the onion, courgettes, flour, beaten eggs, half the cheese and the parsley, adding salt and pepper to taste. Butter a shallow ovenproof dish and fill with the mixture. Place the slices of tomato around the edge and sprinkle over the remaining cheese. Dot with butter and dust with the paprika. Bake for 45 minutes until golden brown and bubbling.

COURGETTE, SWISS CHARD AND FETA FRITTATA

* 1 courgette, grated
* 1 red or green chilli, seeds removed and finely sliced
* 1 egg
* 1 heaped teaspoon gram flour
* 250g Swiss chard, roughly chopped, or 250g spinach
* 60g (vegetarian) feta, crumbled
* handful flat-leafed parsley, roughly chopped
* 1 clove garlic, chopped
* a little salt (the feta will provide some) plus freshly ground black pepper
* olive oil

Mix all the ingredients in a bowl except the olive oil, which you heat in a non-stick frying pan. Pour in the mix and allow to cook on a medium heat for about 6 minutes. Either upturn on to a clean plate and return to the pan to cook the other side for a further 5 minutes or put the pan under the grill to continue cooking until golden brown and puffed up.

ROQUEFORT NIBBLES

This is so quick and easy and can also be made in larger portions 2–3 inch square, to be served as a light lunch with a green or mixed salad.

* 1 pack ready-made all-butter flaky pastry
* 100g Roquefort cheese
* 1 egg, lightly beaten with a splash of water

Preheat the oven to 180°C (fan). Roll out the pastry to a thickness of a pound coin and cut an even number into squares just over 1 inch in size. With the point of a knife, slash the middle of every other pastry square 3 times. Crumble the Roquefort cheese and place about ½ teaspoon in the middle of the other squares. Brush the edges with the beaten egg and place the slashed squares on top, sealing well. Place on a baking tray and brush with the remaining egg wash. Bake for about 6–8 minutes or until puffed up and golden and serve warm.

RATATOUILLE

* 1 courgette, roughly chopped or sliced
* 1 aubergine (250g), roughly chopped or sliced
* 1 red onion, sliced
* 1 red pepper, deseeded and roughly chopped
* 2 cloves garlic, chopped
* 4 ripe tomatoes, roughly chopped
* olive oil
* 4 small non-stick frying pans
* salt and freshly ground black pepper
* basil leaves

Place 4 small frying pans on to heat and drop a good slug (about a tablespoon) of olive oil into each. Put the courgette and aubergine into one, the tomatoes in another, the red pepper in a third and the onion in a fourth. Season each pan with a little salt, bring up to heat, stir, then reduce the heat to a simmer so that each vegetable cooks gently in its own juices without burning, stirring every now and then. When the vegetables are soft, stir in the garlic with the onion. After a couple of minutes, tip the pepper in with the onion, then add the courgette and aubergine, finally the tomatoes. Mix together gently and allow to cool slightly before serving, sprinkled with a few basil leaves. This can be eaten hot, or nearer to room temperature, even chilled with crispy French bread. It also goes well with an omelette and pasta and, by cooking each component individually, you really get to savour the taste of each vegetable.

CRUNCHY TOPPED RUNNER BEAN, COURGETTE AND TOMATO BAKE

  (IF OMITTING BREADCRUMBS)

* 1 courgette, sliced
* 125g runner beans, finely sliced
* 3 tomatoes, sliced
* 1 egg
* 1 tablespoon gram flour
* 2–3 tablespoons grated Parmesan
* 3 tablespoons crème fraîche
* 1 teaspoon Dijon mustard
* 1 slice brown bread, roughly crumbled
* drizzle of olive oil
* salt and freshly ground black pepper

Preheat the oven to 180°C (fan). Lightly boil the runner beans and courgette for 2 minutes. Drain well and lay on the bottom of an ovenproof dish and place the tomatoes on top. In a small bowl, whisk the egg into the gram flour and add the Parmesan, crème fraîche and Dijon mustard, making sure there are no lumps. Season lightly with salt and a few good grinds of black pepper. Pour over the vegetables and spread to cover. Crumble over the breadcrumbs and drizzle with a splash of olive oil. Bake for about 15–20 minutes until bubbling and golden. Serve on its own or with a green salad.

AUBERGINE BAKE

V GF

* 1x 400g tin cherry tomatoes
* 1 aubergine (250g), cut lengthways into slices about 1cm thick or slightly less
* 150g Burrata
* grated Parmesan
* olive oil
* sunflower oil
* fresh basil leaves
* gram flour
* 1 egg, lightly beaten
* salt and freshly ground black pepper

Preheat the oven to 180°C (fan). Begin by laying the aubergine slices on a plate and lightly sprinkle with salt. Leave for ½ hour. In the meantime, tip the tinned cherry tomatoes into a pan and add about a handful of roughly torn basil leaves and a tablespoon of olive oil. Season lightly, bring to the boil and simmer very gently, stirring every now and again, or until the liquid has reduced and it has become slightly jammy. Put several tablespoons of gram flour into a shallow dish and the beaten egg into another. Heat about 2 tablespoons each of the olive oil and sunflower oil in a shallow pan. Wipe off the moisture from the aubergine slices with a piece of kitchen paper, cover each one with the gram flour and dip into the beaten egg. Carefully lay into the hot oil and cook gently for about 2–3 minutes on each side. Lift on to kitchen paper and cook the remaining slices in the same way. Take an ovenproof dish, lay some aubergine slices on the bottom, spoon over some of the tomato sauce, tear the Burrata and scatter over plus a few torn basil leaves, finally grating a tablespoon or so of Parmesan. Repeat once more and finish with a little freshly ground black pepper, salt and a further drizzle of olive oil. Bake until bubbling and brown. Don't serve hot but a bit more than room temperature with a green salad and some crispy bread.

RED AND SPLIT YELLOW LENTIL DHAL

* 100g red lentils
* 100g split yellow lentils
* 1 stick cinnamon
* 8 cardamom pods
* 2 bay leaves, roughly crushed

Soak the lentils in a bowl of cold water for at least 2 hours or overnight. Drain, rinse under a cold tap and place in a pan with the spices and twice the volume of cold water. Bring to the boil, stir, cover and simmer on a very gentle heat until the lentils are soft and most of the cooking liquid is absorbed. Because the yellow lentils cook more slowly than the red variety, this could take at least 40 minutes and you will need to stir fairly frequently to prevent sticking and burning on the bottom. You may also have to add extra water during the cooking.

Note: if you contain the spices in a small square of muslin or a muslin bag it can be removed easily when the lentils are cooked. Only season with salt and pepper once the lentils are cooked.

SPLIT YELLOW LENTILS

This is an easy dish to prepare and can be done in several stages, in your own time. Great on its own with rice, naan bread or poppadoms.

* 100g split yellow lentils
* 1 tablespoon sunflower oil
* 1 large red onion, sliced
* 5cm piece fresh ginger, peeled and grated
* 4 tomatoes, roughly chopped, or 1x 400g tin chopped tomatoes
* 1 red chilli, deseeded and finely sliced
* 2 tablespoons fresh coriander, roughly chopped
* salt and pepper

Soak the lentils in plenty of water overnight. The next day, drain and put into a pan covering them with plenty of fresh water. Bring to the boil and cook for 5 minutes on a high heat before reducing it to a simmer. Stir every now and again and check that there is enough – but not too much – water. Don't add any salt at this stage or the lentils will toughen. They could take a good 40 minutes to soften, maybe even up to an hour, until most of the water has been absorbed. The next stage: heat the oil in a frying pan and cook the onion on a medium heat for 5 minutes. Add the ginger, chilli, tomatoes and coriander and cook for about 5 minutes before adding the lentils. Season well with salt and pepper and simmer very gently for about 15–20 minutes adding more water if necessary.

POTATO-LESS PAKORAS

* 1 carrot, grated
* 1 courgette, grated
* 1 red onion, sliced
* 250g Swiss chard or 250g spinach
* 1 heaped tablespoon gram flour
* 1 green chilli, deseeded and chopped
* ½ teaspoon garam masala
* ½ teaspoon coriander seeds
* ¼ teaspoon dried chilli flakes
* juice ½ lemon
* water
* salt and freshly ground black pepper
* oil for frying

Begin by heating a frying pan and add the spices. Allow them to toast for a minute or two but be careful they don't burn. Grind them in a pestle and mortar enough to crush the coriander seeds. In a bowl, mix the gram flour with the toasted spices and enough water to make a loose batter. Add the vegetables, lemon juice and seasoning and mix everything together with your hands. Heat about 1cm of oil in a non-stick frying pan and gently drop in individual handfuls of the pakora mixture. Allow to cook for about 6 minutes and then gently turn each pakora and cook for a further 6 minutes or more until they are a deep golden brown. Lift from the pan and drain thoroughly on kitchen paper. Serve at room temperature with mango chutney and cucumber raita (see page 82).

VEGETABLE AND PASTA BAKE

V

* Any mix of vegetables you have available. For this, I used:
* 2 leeks, sliced
* 200g Swiss chard, sliced
* 2 courgettes, sliced
* 220g French beans
* 500g fresh pasta
* 350g ready-made cheese sauce
* 4 tablespoons crème fraîche
* 2 tablespoons grated Parmesan cheese
* olive oil (optional)

Preheat the oven to 180°C (fan). Blanch the chard until soft but not cooked, drain and slice. Boil the other vegetables in a little water till almost cooked then drain. Cook the pasta until al dente and drain. In a bowl, mix the cheese sauce with the crème fraîche and add the vegetables and pasta, mixing well. Tip into a buttered ovenproof dish and scatter over the grated Parmesan. Either put to one side in the fridge to be cooked later or bake until bubbling and golden brown. You can add some sliced tomatoes on top before the cheese, drizzling with a little olive oil. A light dusting of fresh brown breadcrumbs adds a nice crunch.

BRAISED WHITE BEANS

This can be prepared the day before and goes very well with lamb or pork.

* 1x 400g tin white haricot beans, rinsed and drained
* 2 slices smoked streaky bacon, cut into smallish pieces
* 2 large tomatoes, chopped, or 1x 200g tin chopped tomatoes
* 1 large shallot, chopped, or 1 red onion, chopped
* 1 tablespoon concentrated tomato purée
* 3 sprigs fresh thyme, leaves only
* 1 sprig rosemary, leaves removed and chopped
* 1 stick celery, sliced
* 2 bay leaves
* 1 clove garlic, crushed

Fry the bacon in a heavy pan until crispy. Add the shallot or onion, stir for a minute and add the tomatoes and all remaining ingredients. Add just enough water to cover, stir and bring to the boil. Reduce the heat and simmer for about ¾ hour checking every now and again adding a little more water if necessary.

ROASTED VEGETABLES WITH AUBERGINE

   (IF OMITTING PARMESAN)

* selection of vegetables of your choice. For example:
* 200g butternut squash, peeled and roughly chopped
* 2 sweet peppers, deseeded and roughly chopped
* 2 red onions, cut into quarters
* 1 sweet potato (250g), peeled and sliced
* 250g swede, peeled and cut into small pieces (this takes longer to cook)
* 1 aubergine (250g)
* olive oil
* garlic
* salt and freshly ground black pepper

Preheat the oven to 180°C (fan). Begin by baking the aubergine whole for about 20–30 minutes depending on size until soft. Cut in half and scoop out the flesh. Leave to cool. Place your selection of vegetables in an ovenproof dish, drizzle over a little olive oil and mix well. Season and dot with several cloves of garlic still in their skin. Roast for about 20 minutes, turning once or twice. Roughly chop the cooked aubergine and stir into the vegetables. Put back into the oven for a further 10 minutes or until the vegetables are starting to scorch.

SOFT AND TASTY AUBERGINES

Although this needs a little planning ahead it is an easy way to cook aubergines without them mopping up large quantities of oil.

For 2

* 2 aubergines (450–500g), cut into slices 1cm thick
* olive oil
* zest and juice 1 lemon
* 1 teaspoon dried mixed herbs
* 1 clove garlic, crushed
* salt and pepper

Place the aubergine slices in a colander, sprinkle with salt and allow to drain over a bowl for at least 1 hour. Rinse thoroughly under cold water and dry in a clean drying-up cloth. Lay the aubergine slices on a sheet of kitchen paper and leave for about 30 minutes to dry. Brush with olive oil, heat a griddle pan and lay the aubergine slices oiled side down and cook for about 3 minutes. Lightly oil the slices and turn to cook for a further 2 minutes. You will probably have to do this in several batches. Place the cooked aubergine slices in a dish. Mix the garlic with a tablespoon of olive oil, the mixed herbs, lemon zest and juice and season with salt and pepper. Add this to the aubergine slices, stirring well, and leave to cool. Serve at room temperature.

SPIRALISED COURGETTE, PINE NUTS, ROASTED ARTICHOKES AND SWEET RED PEPPERS

   (IF OMITTING PARMESAN)

* 1 courgette, spiralised or chopped
* 1 tablespoon pine nuts
* 6 spring onions, sliced
* 1 red pepper, deseeded and roughly chopped
* ⅓ jar roasted artichokes in olive oil, roughly chopped
* 1 clove garlic, crushed
* 1 tablespoon olive oil
* small handful (about 1 tablespoon) basil, roughly torn
* salt and freshly ground black pepper
* freshly grated Parmesan

Begin by heating a non-stick frying pan and quickly toast the pine nuts, making sure they don't burn by shaking the pan. Remove from the pan and put to one side. In the same pan heat a tablespoon of olive oil, add the salad onion/spring onions and sweet peppers and sweat on a medium heat for about 6 minutes, stirring so they don't burn. Put the spiralised courgette into a saucepan with a little salt and barely cover with boiling water. Cook for about 2–3 minutes keeping it al dente. Drain. Add the garlic and artichokes to the other vegetables, stir, season with salt and freshly ground black pepper and thoroughly heat through. Add the torn basil and tip on the drained courgette. Stir, put into a bowl or onto a plate and finish with the grated Parmesan. Serve immediately.

CAULIFLOWER AND CHICKPEA COUSCOUS

* 400g cauliflower
* 4 spring onions, sliced
* 1x 400g tin chickpeas, drained
* ½ teaspoon each:
* ground cinnamon, ground coriander, ground cumin, paprika
* 1 heaped tablespoon sultanas
* 1 heaped tablespoon toasted almonds
* juice 1 orange
* salt and pepper
* olive oil
* small handful fresh coriander

Break up the cauliflower into small florets and blitz in a blender until small crumbs but not puréed. Heat a splash of olive oil in a pan and add the chickpeas. Cook for 3 minutes and put to one side. In another pan, heat one tablespoon olive oil and add the cauliflower and spices. Stir for a minute or so and add the sultanas, toasted almonds and spring onions. Season well and stir in the roughly chopped fresh coriander. Serve immediately.

MACARONI, LEEK, RED PEPPER AND TOMATO BAKE

* 200g dry macaroni
* 2 leeks, sliced
* 1 long, sweet red pepper, deseeded and sliced
* 1 tomato, roughly chopped
* 150g strong Cheddar cheese, grated plus a little extra for the top
* 1 tablespoon butter
* 1 tablespoon gram flour
* 1 heaped tablespoon crème fraîche
* 1 teaspoon Dijon mustard
* 1 dessertspoon panko crumbs
* salt and pepper

Preheat the oven to 180°C (fan). Put the macaroni on to cook in a pan with salted boiling water making sure you stir to prevent the pasta from sticking to the bottom. When cooked, drain and reserve the pasta water. Put the leeks and pepper in a pan with half the butter and some of the pasta water. Bring to the boil and gently simmer, stirring once in a while. When both the vegetables and leeks are cooked, mix the pasta with the vegetables, keeping the cooking juices. Melt the remaining butter in a pan with the gram flour and whisk in some of the remaining pasta water. Bring to the boil, stirring all the while, then remove from the heat and stir in the crème fraîche, cheese and mustard. Season well and pour into a shallow gratin dish. Scatter some more grated cheese on the top along with the panko breadcrumbs. Bake until browned and bubbling.

BROCCOLI, CAULIFLOWER AND CHICKPEA GRATIN

* 400g cauliflower, broken into florets
* 250g broccoli, broken into florets
* 1x 400g tin chickpeas, drained and rinsed
* 1 heaped tablespoon gram flour
* 30g butter
* 275ml milk
* 3 tablespoons crème fraîche
* 60g Gruyère cheese, grated
* 1 teaspoon Dijon mustard
* 1 heaped tablespoon panko crumbs
* ¼ teaspoon freshly grated nutmeg
* salt and pepper

Steam the cauliflower with the broccoli for 5–6 minutes but keeping a bit of crunch. Make the cheese sauce by melting the butter with the gram flour in a non-stick pan. Bring to the boil, stirring all the while and gradually whisk in the mustard and milk to avoid lumps until it boils and has thickened. Remove from the heat and add the cheese, the crème fraîche and freshly grated nutmeg. Arrange the cauliflower and broccoli in an ovenproof dish and scatter over the chickpeas. Pour on the cheese sauce and sprinkle with the panko crumbs and a little more grated cheese. If using straight away, place under a hot grill until bubbling and brown. If not, reheat in a hot oven (180°C fan) for about 15 minutes and serve on its own or with a green salad.

CAULIFLOWER AND KALE GRATIN

* 200g kale
* 800g cauliflower, cut into florets
* 1 tablespoon plain flour
* 1 tablespoon butter
* 110ml milk
* 60g grated Gruyère cheese
* 1 teaspoon Dijon mustard
* 1 tablespoon crème fraîche
* salt and pepper
* freshly grated nutmeg

Preheat the oven to 180°C (fan). Cook the cauliflower and kale in a pan with a little boiling water until there is still a little crunch, drain and place in a shallow ovenproof dish. Make the cheese sauce by melting the butter and flour in a pan. Stir and cook for a minute before whisking in the mustard and milk. Bring to the boil and stir until thickened. Remove from the heat and add the cheese and grated nutmeg.

Add salt and pepper to taste. Pour over the vegetables and scatter a little more cheese on top. Bake for 15 minutes or until bubbling and golden.

FISH

COLD SAUCE FOR FISH (1)

* 2 spring onions, sliced
* 1 tablespoon natural yoghurt
* 1 tablespoon good-quality mayonnaise
* 1 tablespoon chopped parsley
* salt and pepper
* juice ½ lemon

Mix everything together and drizzle over the fish and accompanying salad of tomatoes or cucumber etc. and serve.

COLD SAUCE FOR FISH (2)

* 1 tablespoon natural yoghurt
* 1 teaspoon dill, chopped
* 1 teaspoon capers, roughly chopped
* 1 tablespoon green pepper, finely chopped
* 2 spring onions, finely sliced
* salt and freshly ground black pepper

Mix everything together and serve with fried or poached fish, hot or cold.

POACHED SMOKED HADDOCK

* 1x 130g undyed smoked haddock
* 60g kale, roughly chopped
* 2–3 carrots, cut into batons
* 1 leek, sliced
* soy
* milk

Poach the haddock in a little milk for about 5 minutes. Cook the kale, carrot batons and leek in a wok with a little soy and water and serve with the haddock.

KEDGEREE

* 350g undyed smoked haddock, poached in a little milk for 6–8 minutes
* 100g wholegrain basmati rice, cooked according to pack instructions
* 1 red onion, finely sliced
* 100g each:
* frozen edamame and baby broad beans and petits pois
* 1 hard-boiled egg, sliced
* ½ red, green, orange or yellow pepper, chopped
* good handful fresh coriander and parsley, chopped
* good pinch cayenne pepper
* zest and juice ½ lemon
* a little olive oil

Preheat the oven to 180°C (fan). Remove the skin from the haddock and flake the fish onto a separate dish, removing any bones. Spray a small frying pan two or three times with a low-calorie olive oil and add the finely sliced red onion. Cover with a little boiling water and simmer, stirring until the liquid has evaporated and the onion has begun to turn golden brown. Put the frozen vegetables and the pepper into a pan with a little boiling water and cook for about 5 minutes. Drain and gently fold in the other ingredients except the fried onion and lemon. Sprinkle with the zest and juice of the lemon, scatter over the fried onion and drizzle with a little olive oil. Cover with foil and bake until piping hot.

BAKED HAKE AND VEGETABLES

* 1x 130g hake fillets
* juice ½ lemon
* salt and pepper

Preheat the oven to 180˚C (fan). Place the fillet of hake in a shallow ovenproof dish. Splash with the lemon juice and season with salt and pepper. Bake for about 8 minutes, or until the fish is cooked through. Serve with a green vegetable, either stir-fried in a very little oil or steamed.

HADDOCK WITH SWEET POTATO ROSTI

* 1x 130g frozen haddock
* 1 courgette, grated
* 1 small sweet potato (130g), peeled and grated
* a little virgin olive oil plus low-calorie spray olive oil
* 2 carrots, scrubbed, sliced and steamed
* 6 cherry tomatoes, roasted
* salt and freshly ground black pepper

Preheat the oven to 180˚C (fan). Place the haddock in a small ovenproof dish with the tomatoes. Drizzle with a little olive oil and bake for about 15 minutes. Mix the courgette and sweet potato in a bowl and season well with salt and freshly ground black pepper. Spray a non-stick frying pan and tip in the rosti mix. Cook gently for about 6 minutes. Place a plate on the pan and tip out the rosti, then slide it back into the pan and cook until soft in the centre. Serve with the roasted tomatoes and fish and steamed carrots.

HOT SMOKED SALMON FILLETS

* 265g salmon
* 1 tablespoon white rice grains
* 1 tablespoon soft brown sugar
* 2 teabags of tea: Earl Grey, jasmine, green or black tea of your choice, emptied
* aluminium foil

FOR THE FISH MARINADE:

* 1 small teaspoon runny honey
* 1 clove garlic, crushed
* pinch chilli flakes or ½ small red or green chilli, deseeded and finely chopped
* 1 tablespoon soy
* 5cm piece freshly grated ginger

Marinate the salmon in the sauce for at least ½ hour. Using an old wok or small ovenproof dish, place a crumpled piece of foil on the bottom and add the mix of tea, sugar and rice. Put on a moderate heat on the stove and when it starts to smoke, place over a small rack on which you lay the fish. Cover tightly with more foil and cook on a moderate to low heat for about 12 minutes, or until the fish is cooked through. Either serve hot or cold.

HOT SMOKED SALMON SALAD

* Mix gently together:
* 150g hot smoked salmon
* 1 fennel bulb, sliced
* 6 radishes, washed, trimmed and sliced
* 1 avocado, sliced
* 30g mint, chopped
* juice 1 lemon
* 2 tablespoons yoghurt
* 1 tablespoons mayonnaise
* salt and pepper

HOT SMOKED SALMON AND BLACK BEAN GALETTE

DF GF

* 150g hot smoked salmon
* ½x 400g tin black beans, drained and rinsed
* 1 small or ½ courgette, finely chopped
* 1x 160g tin sweetcorn, drained
* 1 small red onion, finely chopped
* 1 red chilli, deseeded and finely chopped
* handful parsley, chopped
* 1 level tablespoon gram flour
* 1 egg
* zest 1 small lemon
* ½ fennel bulb, finely chopped
* salt and freshly ground black pepper
* oil for frying

Put the black beans into a bowl and lightly crush. Add the egg, gram flour, red onion, parsley, chilli, lemon zest, fennel, sweetcorn and courgette and mix well together. Add the hot smoked salmon, gently flaking it with your fingers and fold in with the salt and pepper. Heat a very little oil in a small non-stick frying pan and tip in the mixture. Flatten it slightly, reduce the heat to medium and allow to cook for about 5 minutes. Take a plate the size of the pan and place on top reversing it so that the galette turns out onto the plate. Put the pan back on the heat and slide the galette back into the pan to continue cooking for a further 3–4 minutes. Serve with a wedge of lemon and a salad or vegetable of your choice. Baked tomatoes would be good.

SALMON BAKED WITH FENNEL, TOMATO AND CHILLI

DF GF

* 130g salmon
* 1 fennel bulb, finely sliced
* 1 large, ripe beef tomato, sliced
* 1 clove garlic, crushed
* 1 small chilli, deseeded and finely chopped
* juice ½ large lemon
* salt and freshly ground black pepper

Preheat the oven to 180°C (fan). Lay the sliced tomato on the base of an ovenproof dish. Lightly steam the fennel until half cooked and scatter over the tomato. Place the salmon on top and scatter over the garlic and chilli. Sprinkle over the lemon juice and season with salt and pepper. Bake for about 10–15 minutes until the fish is cooked through.

FISHCAKES

* 130g frozen haddock
* ½x 400g tin chickpeas, drained, rinsed and lightly crushed
* 100g watercress, thoroughly washed and roughly chopped
* 1 courgette, grated
* zest ½ lemon
* 1 egg
* 1 tablespoon gram flour
* salt and pepper
* 2 spring onions, finely sliced
* ½ small green chilli, deseeded and finely sliced
* milk

Preheat the oven to 180°C (fan). Bake the haddock from frozen in enough milk just to cover it. This will take about 10 minutes. Drain and allow to cool, removing skin if necessary and add to all the other ingredients. Flatten the mixture in the bowl and cut into quarters. Take each quarter one at a time and shape into balls, place on a dish and slightly flatten. Keep in the fridge until ready to cook either by shallow-frying in a pan or by baking in the oven for 10 minutes (having first lightly sprayed the fishcakes with oil).

CRAB CAKES

* 100g fresh cooked white crabmeat
* 1 small or ½ red chilli, deseeded and finely chopped
* 1 slice multi-seeded bread, crumbled
* zest ½ lime
* 5cm piece fresh ginger, grated
* 1 tablespoon fresh coriander (including stalks), roughly chopped
* salt and freshly ground black pepper
* gram flour
* soy
* salad leaves (lettuce, rocket)

Mix together the crab, chilli, breadcrumbs, lime zest, ginger, coriander, salt and pepper and shape into cakes. Cover with gram flour and set in the fridge for at least an hour before shallow-frying in a little sunflower, rape or vegetable oil. Drizzle with a little soy and serve with the salad leaves and lime wedges.

CRAB AND SWEETCORN PATTY – SIMILAR TO CRAB CAKES BUT SLIGHTLY DIFFERENT

* 100g fresh cooked white crab meat
* 1 fresh corn cob, outer husks discarded, kernels stripped (or 1x 160g tin unsweetened corn)
* 1 slice multi-seeded bread or wholemeal bread, crumbled
* 1 tablespoon cashew nuts, broken into small pieces with a rolling pin
* zest and juice 1 lemon
* 1 clove garlic, crushed
* 1 egg, lightly beaten
* ½ red chilli, deseeded and finely chopped
* 5cm piece fresh ginger, grated
* 3 spring onions, sliced
* small handful (about 1 tablespoon when roughly chopped) coriander and/or parsley/chervil
* fine polenta

Mix everything together but the polenta and shape into two cakes. Cover with the polenta by spooning it over the cakes, pressing gently as they are very fragile. Leave in the fridge for at least 1 hour to settle. Heat a little vegetable or sunflower oil in a non-stick frying pan and carefully place the crab cakes. After about 4 minutes on a medium heat, turn them and cook for a further 3 minutes.

HADDOCK RAGOUT

* 130g fillet frozen haddock
* 6 cherry tomatoes, halved
* 1 small red onion, sliced
* 1 clove garlic, chopped
* 1 tablespoon olive oil
* 1 tablespoon Worcestershire sauce
* salt and pepper

Heat the oil in a pan and add the sliced onion. Sweat for a minute and add the tomatoes. Cook for 3 minutes then add the Worcestershire sauce, garlic and fish and season lightly with salt and pepper. Spoon the juices over the fish and cover the pan with a lid. Simmer gently until the onion is completely soft and the fish cooked through. Serve with plain boiled rice and a green vegetable.

SALMON WITH SWEET CHILLI JELLY

* 130g salmon, skin off
* 1 teaspoon sweet chilli jelly
* 1 small or ½ chilli of your choice, seeds removed and finely sliced
* juice ½ lemon
* 1 small clove garlic, crushed
* 5cm piece root ginger, grated
* 1 teaspoon soy

Preheat the oven to 180°C (fan). Place the salmon in a small ovenproof dish. Mix all the marinade ingredients and spoon over the fish. Bake for approximately 10 minutes. Serve with vegetables of your choice.

SALMON EN PAPILLOTE WITH HUMMUS AND DILL

* 130g salmon (can be cooked from frozen)
* juice ½ lemon plus 1 slice
* few fronds of fresh dill
* 1 tablespoon homemade hummus (see page 76)
* few grinds roasted garlic and pepper (available with the spices and condiments at most supermarkets)
* baking parchment

Preheat the oven to 180°C (fan). Lay the salmon on the baking parchment and spread with the hummus. Scatter the dill, add the lemon juice and slice cut in two and sprinkle with a few grinds of the roasted garlic and pepper. Place the long sides of the parchment together and fold several times, leaving a little room about the fish. Scrunch up each end and twist to close the parcel. Bake on a metal tray or in a small dish for about 10 minutes – the frozen fish will take longer to cook. Serve immediately with a vegetable of your choice or a salad.

SALMON BAKED WITH FENNEL, TOMATO AND CHILLI

DF GF

* 130g salmon
* 1 fennel bulb, finely sliced
* 1 large ripe beef tomato, sliced
* 1 clove garlic, crushed
* 1 small chilli, deseeded and finely chopped
* juice ½ large lemon
* salt and freshly ground black pepper

Preheat the oven to 180°C (fan). Lay the sliced tomato on the base of an ovenproof dish. Lightly steam the fennel until half cooked and scatter over the tomato. Place the salmon on top and scatter over the garlic and chilli. Sprinkle over the lemon juice and season with salt and pepper. Bake for about 10–15 minutes until the fish is cooked through.

SMOKED AND FRESH HADDOCK BAKED WITH FENNEL, TOMATO AND ONION

DF GF

* 130g haddock
* 130g smoked haddock
* 1 tomato, sliced
* 1 red onion, finely sliced
* ½ fennel bulb, finely sliced
* ½ teaspoon fennel seeds
* 1–2 cloves of garlic, crushed
* 1 tablespoon olive oil
* small handful fresh parsley, roughly chopped
* salt and freshly ground black pepper
* lemon wedges for serving

Preheat the oven to 180°C (fan). Thaw the fish and put to one side. Place the fennel, onion and tomato in a medium shallow ovenproof dish, drizzle with the olive oil and bake for about 20 minutes or until nearly cooked through. Cut the fish into chunks and place on top. Scatter over the fennel seeds and garlic and season with salt and pepper. Add a dash of water if necessary or a little more olive oil and spoon over the fish. Return to the oven and bake for a further 10 minutes. Serve with lemon wedges and lots of parsley on a bed of quinoa or rice of your choice.

BAKED SALMON WITH BELUGA LENTILS

(DF) (GF)

* 130g salmon (if frozen, thaw first)
* 1 pouch ready-cooked Beluga lentils
* soy
* juice 1 lemon
* 1 small clove garlic, crushed
* 100g kalettes (a cross between sprouts and kale and available in supermarkets)
* 125g asparagus tips
* 1 leek, finely sliced

Preheat the oven to 180°C (fan). Place the salmon in a small ovenproof dish and sprinkle over the soy, garlic and lemon juice. Bake for about 6–8 minutes. Serve with the hot lentils and steamed asparagus and kalettes.

SMOKED MACKEREL SALAD

(DF) (GF)

* 100g smoked mackerel, skin removed and flaked
* 1 stick celery, sliced
* 2 spring onions, sliced
* several leaves red radicchio, roughly torn
* ½ fennel bulb, finely sliced
* small handful fresh dill and basil leaves
* juice ½ lemon
* 1 tablespoon mayonnaise
* 1 tablespoon natural yoghurt
* salt and pepper

Put the fish and vegetables into a pretty bowl and dress with the mayonnaise and yoghurt. The addition of ½ crispy eating apple would be nice and, possibly, some sunflower and pumpkin seeds.

SMOKED MACKEREL, EGG AND BEETROOT SALAD

(DF) (IF OMITTING YOGHURT) (GF)

* 100g smoked mackerel, skin removed and flaked
* 1 hard-boiled egg, sliced or cut into wedges
* 1 cooked beetroot, roughly chopped
* several leaves red radicchio, torn into pieces
* 1 fennel bulb, thinly sliced
* 6 radishes, washed, trimmed and thinly sliced
* 3 spring onions, sliced
* 1 tablespoon each of sunflower and pumpkin seeds

Lay the above ingredients in scattered layers on a pretty serving dish starting with the radicchio leaves.

Dress with natural yoghurt mixed with a spoonful of mayonnaise and the juice of ½ lemon, salt and pepper.

SMOKED TROUT PATE

(GF)

* 265g smoked trout fillets
* 1 tablespoon good-quality mayonnaise
* 1 tablespoon natural yoghurt
* ½ teaspoon horseradish cream
* juice 1 lemon
* salt and freshly ground black pepper

Pulse everything quickly in a small blender and spoon into a pretty dish.

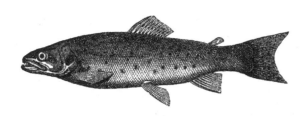

SARDINE SALAD

GF

* 1x 135g tin sardines in olive oil, drained
* 1 cooked beetroot, roughly chopped
* 1 fennel bulb, finely sliced
* 6 radishes, washed, trimmed and sliced
* 1 tablespoon of mixed seeds (sunflower, pumpkin)
* 6 cherry tomatoes, cut in half
* 1 avocado, sliced
* 30g slice feta, crumbled
* juice ½ lemon
* 1 tablespoon olive oil
* 1 tablespoon cider vinegar
* salt and freshly ground black pepper

Lay the sardines, vegetables, mixed seeds and feta on a pretty dish and drizzle with the olive oil, lemon juice and cider vinegar. Season with salt and freshly ground black pepper.

SALMON BAKED IN PARCHMENT

DF GF

* 130g salmon steak per person
* 1 pouch ready-cooked brown basmati rice
* 1x 400g tin chickpeas, drained and rinsed
* soy
* 1 lemon
* garlic
* vegetable oil

Preheat the oven to 180°C (fan). Place the salmon on a large piece of baking parchment, dot with chopped garlic and squeeze the juice from ½ a lemon. Splash with a very little soy and fold the parchment to make a sealed package. Place on a metal baking sheet and bake for about 6 minutes. Heat the rice and chickpeas according to pack instructions. Serve with the fish on top of the rice/chickpeas and a green vegetable plus the other half of the lemon.

SARDINES ON TOAST

DF **GF** (IF USING GLUTEN-FREE BREAD)

* 2 sardines from a 1x 135g tin in olive oil
* 1 slice bread of your choice
* ½ avocado, sliced
* little gem lettuce heart
* 2 small tomatoes, sliced
* Greek basil leaves, roughly torn
* juice ½ lemon
* 1 clove garlic, crushed
* salt and pepper

Toast the bread and rub with the garlic. Lightly mash the sardines and spread on top. Serve with the avocado, tomatoes and lettuce with a dressing of lemon juice and a splash of olive oil.

BAKED HADDOCK WITH ZINGY CREME FRAICHE AND CHEESE TOPPING

This is for one person but easily adapted for more.

GF

* 130g frozen or fresh haddock
* 250g spinach
* 6 cherry tomatoes, cut in half
* 2 tablespoons crème fraîche
* zest ½ lemon plus juice
* 1 heaped tablespoon pecorino* (or Parmesan)
* 30g slice feta
* small handful fresh sweet or Greek basil leaves, roughly chopped
* olive oil
* salt and freshly ground black pepper

Preheat the oven to 180°C (fan). You can cook the fish from frozen but it will take a little longer so generally, I thaw first. Wilt the spinach in a pan with a dash of boiling water then drain, pressing out as much of the liquid as possible. Spread in the middle of a small ovenproof dish and place the fish on top. Mix together in a small bowl the crème fraîche, lemon zest and pecorino/Parmesan and spread over the fish. Tumble in the tomatoes, crumble the feta cheese and scatter over everything, lastly sprinkling the basil. Lightly season with salt* but give several grinds of pepper. Drizzle lightly with olive oil and lemon juice and bake for about 8–10 minutes or until the fish is thoroughly cooked.

*If using pecorino, this can be quite a bit saltier than Parmesan.

HADDOCK POACHED IN MILK WITH LEEKS AND CARROTS

* 130g haddock
* 1 carrot, peeled and cut into julienne strips
* 1 leek, sliced
* 2 tablespoons milk
* 1 teaspoon olive oil
* Greek basil leaves

Preheat the oven to 180˚C (fan). Put the carrots and leeks in a small ovenproof dish with the olive oil and about 2 tablespoons milk and put into a moderately hot oven, middle shelf. After 8 minutes take out the carrots and leeks. Stir in the milk and snuggle in the frozen fish fillet basting with the juices and covering it with some of the vegetables. Season, sprinkle over some Greek basil leaves and return to the oven for a further 8 minutes or until the fish is cooked through.

HADDOCK WITH BABY VEG STEW

* 130g haddock
* 250g selection of baby vegetables. Mine were what I could forage from the garden and the fridge:
* 1 courgette, sliced
* 80g French beans, sliced
* 80g mangetout, sliced
* 3 Swiss chard leaves, torn
* 80g podded broad beans
* 1 red onion or 3 spring onions, sliced
* 1 clove garlic, crushed
* 3 tomatoes, roughly chopped
* small handful parsley, roughly chopped
* juice 1 lemon
* 1 teaspoon olive oil
* salt and freshly ground black pepper

Heat the olive oil gently in a wok and add the red onion. Stir and cook for 2 minutes then add the other vegetables and cook for 2–3 minutes, stirring every now and then. Add a splash of water and the lemon juice and snuggle in the haddock. Spoon over some of the juices, cover again and cook for 3 minutes. If using frozen fish, as I did, it will take a little longer to cook through, so turn it over and baste it again, stirring in the parsley. Season with salt and freshly ground black pepper and serve at once.

HADDOCK WITH CUCUMBER AND CAPERS

DF **GF**

* 130g haddock fillet
* ½ cucumber, sliced to the thickness of a pound coin piece
* 3 spring onions, sliced or:
* 1 white salad onion, sliced
* 1 teaspoon butter
* 1 tablespoon flat-leafed parsley, roughly chopped
* juice ½ lemon
* 1 teaspoon capers, roughly chopped
* roasted garlic and pepper in its own grinder (available in supermarkets) or:
* 1 clove garlic, crushed
* salt and freshly ground black pepper

Melt the butter in a non-stick frying pan and add the cucumber and onion. Stir and cook for about 3 minutes. Add the fish, remembering it will take longer if cooked from frozen, in which case, reduce the heat to medium so that it won't burn and will cook through. Turn the fish and cook the following side, stirring the cucumber and onion. Add the lemon juice, parsley and capers plus a few grinds of the roasted garlic and pepper – if not available add the fresh garlic now. Continue on a medium heat until the fish is thoroughly cooked.

TROUT WITH ORANGE, HONEY AND THYME

DF (IF OMITTING BUTTER AND USING OIL) **GF**

* 265g trout fillets
* zest ½ orange
* juice ½ lemon
* few sprigs fresh thyme, leaves only, chopped
* 1 teaspoon butter
* ½ teaspoon honey
* salt and pepper

Preheat the oven to 180°C (fan). Mix all the ingredients bar the fish. Put the fillets into a shallow baking dish and dot with the mixture. Bake for about 8 minutes or until cooked. Serve with a vegetable of your choice.

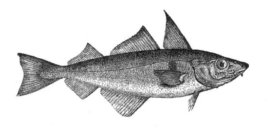

SMOKED HADDOCK AND BUTTER BEAN FISHCAKES

* 140g undyed smoked haddock
* milk
* 1x 400g tin butter beans, rinsed and drained
* good handful parsley, roughly chopped
* 2 spring onions, sliced
* 5cm piece fresh turmeric, peeled and finely grated
* ½ green chilli, deseeded and chopped
* zest and juice ½ lemon
* 1 egg
* panko breadcrumbs
* gram flour
* salt and freshly ground black pepper

Preheat the oven to 180°C (fan). Begin by poaching the haddock in a small dish with enough milk to nearly cover it for about 10 minutes. Remove the skin and any bones and flake with a fork. In a bowl, mash the butter beans. It doesn't matter if they remain uneven and a bit lumpy. Add the parsley, spring onions, chilli, turmeric, lemon juice and zest and season well with salt and lots of freshly ground black pepper. Mix in the flaked haddock and divide into four equal portions which you shape into round cakes about 3cm thick. Beat the egg in a small bowl, put the panko crumbs into another, the gram flour into a third. With one hand take a fishcake and coat it in the gram flour then, using the other hand, roll it in the egg and place in the bowl with the panko crumbs. Use the 'dry' hand to coat the cake and set to one side. Repeat the process until all the cakes are covered in crumbs. These can sit happily in the fridge until needed. Either shallow-fry in a pan with sunflower or vegetable oil until brown on both sides and heated right through or place on a metal oven sheet, spray lightly with low-calorie oil and bake for about 10–15 minutes. Serve with a green vegetable, baked tomatoes and lemon wedges. TIP: when egg-and-breadcrumbing keep one hand for 'dry', the other for 'wet'.

BAKED HADDOCK WITH CARROT AND MIXED SEEDS SALAD

* 130g haddock, skin removed if necessary
* 250g baby spinach
* 1 ripe tomato, finely sliced
* 2 spring onions, finely sliced
* 1 clove garlic, crushed
* juice ½ lemon
* dash Worcestershire sauce
* 1 tablespoon olive oil
* pinch dried chilli flakes

Preheat the oven to 180°C (fan). Steam the spinach and drain thoroughly. Place in a shallow, ovenproof dish and put the fish on top. Position the sliced tomatoes around the edge and scatter over the spring onions, garlic and chilli flakes. Drizzle over the olive oil, lemon juice and Worcestershire sauce and season with salt and freshly ground black pepper. Bake until cooked through and bubbling. Serve with:

CARROT AND MIXED SEED SALAD

* 2 carrots, grated
* juice 1 lemon
* salt and freshly ground black pepper
* 1 teaspoon vegetable or sunflower oil
* 1 teaspoon black onion seeds
* 1 teaspoon mustard seeds
* 1 teaspoon nigella seeds
* a leaf or two fresh coriander to decorate (optional)

Heat the oil in a non-stick frying pan, add the seeds, cover and cook for a brief minute, shaking the pan. When you hear them begin to 'pop' remove from the heat and pour over the carrots. Add the lemon juice and seasoning and stir. Decorate with the coriander.

SIMPLE BAKED SALMON WITH LEEKS, TOMATOES AND RADISHES

(DF) (GF)

* 130g salmon, skin removed
* 1 leek, sliced
* 4 radishes, washed, trimmed and sliced
* 6 cherry tomatoes, cut in half
* 1 clove garlic, crushed
* few sprigs parsley, chopped
* olive oil
* juice ½ lemon
* salt and freshly ground black pepper

Preheat the oven to 180°C (fan). Place the leek, tomatoes, radishes, parsley and garlic into a shallow ovenproof dish. Sprinkle with a little olive oil, season lightly with salt and freshly ground black pepper and bake for about 15 minutes. Place the salmon on top, add a splash more olive oil and the lemon juice and baste the fish before very lightly seasoning it with a little salt. Return to the oven for a further 8–10 minutes. Serve immediately.

PRAWN AND EGG NOODLE STIR-FRY

(GF) (IF OMITTING EGG NOODLES AND USING EDAMAME NOODLES)

* 1 nest medium egg noodles, cooked according to pack instructions
* 150g North Atlantic cold-water prawns – fresh or frozen (thawed)
* ½ each of green, red and yellow peppers, deseeded and finely chopped
* 6 radishes, washed, trimmed and sliced
* 1 clove garlic, chopped
* 3cm piece root ginger, peeled and grated
* 1 tablespoon vegetable oil
* soy
* toasted sesame oil
* 100g frozen petits pois
* fresh coriander

Heat the vegetable oil in a wok and add the vegetables. Stir and cook for 2 minutes before adding the noodles and garlic. Cook a further 2 minutes and add the prawns. Stir in a good splash of soy and cook long enough to heat the prawns thoroughly – about 1–2 minutes. Don't overcook them or they will become tough. Take off the heat, stir in a very small drizzle of the toasted sesame oil, sprinkle with coriander and serve immediately.

PRAWN AND MELON SALAD

GF

* 150g North Atlantic cold-water prawns
* 1 ripe melon (cantaloupe or ogen), cut into small chunks or use a melon baller if you have one
* 3 tablespoons natural yoghurt
* 2 tablespoons good mayonnaise
* juice 1 lemon
* 3–4 shakes of Tabasco
* salt and freshly ground black pepper
* paprika
* 1 pack cress
* 1 little gem lettuce

Mix together the prawns, yoghurt, mayonnaise, melon, lemon juice, Tabasco and seasoning. Serve on the lettuce leaves, dust with a little paprika passed through a tea strainer and scatter over the cress.

MIXED VEGETABLE AND PRAWN STIR-FRY

For 2

* 150g North Atlantic cold-water prawns
* 300g any mix of vegetables. I included: kohlrabi, cucumber, carrot, celery, leek, giant radish, courgette and 2 leaves Swiss chard stripped from the stalks and torn into rough pieces
* 1 clove garlic, chopped
* 2 nests wholewheat egg noodles, cooked according to pack instructions
* 1 tablespoon soy
* vegetable or sunflower oil
* toasted sesame oil
* fresh coriander leaves

Prepare each vegetable into small pieces, either matchsticks, finely sliced or spiralised so that they cook quickly at the same time. Heat a tablespoon of vegetable or sunflower oil in a wok and add all the vegetables except the chard. Stir and cook for 3 minutes. Add the noodles and chard. Stir and cook until the chard has wilted. Add the prawns, the chopped garlic and a couple of good splashes of soy. Cook a further minute so that the prawns are heated through but not cooked further or they will be tough, stir in a very light splash (about 1 teaspoon) of toasted sesame oil and either serve straight from the wok or tip into a pretty bowl, sprinkling over a few fresh coriander leaves.

GIANT PRAWN STIR-FRY WITH SUGAR SNAP PEAS AND KALE

* 180g extra large raw king prawns
* 160g sugar snap peas
* 150g kale
* 1 clove garlic, chopped
* soy
* sunflower or vegetable oil
* small handful coriander, roughly chopped
* juice ½ lemon

Open the prawns along the back and remove any intestinal tract. Place in a dish with the garlic, a dash of soy, half the oil and the lemon juice. Heat a wok and add the remaining oil and then the vegetables. Stir, cover and cook for about 2 minutes, adding a little water if necessary to prevent burning. Add the prawns and the marinade, stir and cook until the prawns turn pink and are cooked through. Season with a little more soy, scatter over the coriander and serve immediately.

GIANT PRAWN AND VEGETABLE STIR-FRY

DF GF

* 180g extra large raw king prawns
* 200g baby spinach, washed
* 160g sugar snap peas, sliced
* 125g asparagus tips, sliced
* 1 clove garlic, chopped
* 3cm piece root ginger, peeled and grated
* 1 chilli, deseeded and finely sliced
* 1 red salad onion or 4 spring onions, sliced
* 1 tablespoon unsalted cashews, roughly chopped
* sunflower oil
* soy
* toasted sesame oil
* handful of fresh coriander, roughly chopped

Heat a tablespoon of sunflower oil in a wok and quickly stir-fry the prawns until they turn pink. Remove and keep to one side. Add a further tablespoon of sunflower oil to the wok and tip in all the vegetables, garlic and cashews. Stir and cover for a minute or so. Remove the lid, stir and add a dash of soy. You may need to add a splash of water at this point to stop the vegetables from burning. Continue stirring until they are nearly cooked and return the prawns plus the coriander. Stir for a minute, sprinkle on a little toasted sesame oil and serve at once.

GIANT PRAWN, BEAN, PEA AND RICE NOODLE STIR-FRY

For 2

* 180g extra large raw king prawns
* 2 nests rice noodles, cooked according to pack instructions*
* 3cm piece of fresh ginger, peeled and grated
* 1 chilli, deseeded and sliced
* juice 1 lemon
* 1 tablespoon soy
* 1 clove garlic, chopped
* a little vegetable oil
* toasted sesame oil
* small handful coriander, roughly chopped
* 150g freshly podded peas (or frozen)
* 100g French beans, sliced

Put the prawns in a dish with the ginger, garlic, soy, lemon juice and chilli and leave to marinate in the fridge for 30 minutes. Heat a tablespoon of oil in a wok and add the peas and beans. Stir, add a dash of water, cover and cook for 2–3 minutes. Remove the lid and add the prawns along with the marinade and cook until the prawns turn pink – about 2 minutes. Tip in the cooked noodles, add a further dash of soy and allow the noodles to heat through for about a minute. Splash on a drizzle of toasted sesame oil (this is for flavour), sprinkle with the coriander and serve immediately.

*Note: as an alternative but higher in calories, substitute the rice noodles for ready-to-use Singapore noodles.

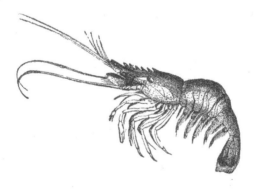

GIANT PRAWN, FRENCH BEAN, CUCUMBER AND CHILLI STIR-FRY

* 180g extra large raw king prawns
* 220g French beans, sliced
* ½ cucumber, cut into batons
* 1 clove garlic, chopped
* 1 nest wholewheat noodles, cooked according to pack instructions
* 1 red chilli, deseeded and finely sliced
* 3cm piece fresh ginger, peeled and grated
* 1 tablespoon vegetable oil
* soy
* toasted sesame oil

Heat the vegetable oil in a wok and add the beans and cucumber. Stir and cook for 3 minutes. Add a splash of water (about 2 tablespoons) and cover. Cook for a further 2 minutes. Remove the lid, stir in the garlic, ginger, chilli, raw prawns and noodles and cook for another 2 minutes or until the prawns have turned pink and the noodles are heated through. Add 2 or 3 shakes of soy, then a very small amount of toasted sesame oil and serve immediately.

GIANT PRAWN AND CARROT STIR-FRY

* 180g extra large raw king prawns
* juice ½ lemon
* 3cm piece root ginger, peeled and grated
* 1 small red chilli, deseeded and finely sliced
* 1 clove garlic, crushed
* soy
* 60g organic, gluten-free edamame noodles, cooked according to pack instructions
* 2 large carrots, cut into small batons
* 6 radishes, washed, trimmed and sliced
* small handful fresh coriander, roughly chopped
* vegetable or sunflower oil

Mix the lemon juice, ginger, garlic and soy in a small bowl and add the prawns. Allow to rest in the fridge for about 10 minutes. Heat a teaspoon of oil in a wok and add the carrots and radishes. Stir for a minute, add a little water and allow to cook until the liquid has almost evaporated. Add the prawns plus the marinade and the noodles and stir-fry for 3–4 minutes. Serve with a sprinkling of fresh coriander leaves.

VIRTUALLY GUILT-FREE PRAWN COCKTAIL

For 2

* 180g North Atlantic cold-water prawns
* 1 tablespoon half-fat crème fraîche
* 1 tablespoon natural yoghurt
* juice ½ lemon
* lettuce, such as little gem, washed and sliced
* 1 teaspoon tomato ketchup
* 1–2 dashes Tabasco sauce
* salt and freshly ground black pepper
* paprika for dusting

Slice the lettuce and pile it into a pretty dish or jar. Mix the crème fraîche, yoghurt, lemon juice, Tabasco, tomato ketchup, salt and freshly ground black pepper and fold in the prawns. Pile these on top of the lettuce and sprinkle with a dusting of paprika passed through a fine tea strainer.

BABY SARDINES WITH MICROGREENS AND SALAD LEAVES

* 1x 135g tin Parmentier's *petites sardines aux deux olives* (or other sardines)
* 50g pea shoots (or substitute with 50g watercress)
* 50g microgreens (or substitute with 50g watercress)
* 50g baby sorrel leaves (or substitute with 50g watercress)
* chives
* 120g salad leaves with rocket
* juice 1 lemon
* 1 tablespoon olive oil
* salt and pepper

Make the dressing by whisking the lemon juice, olive oil, salt and pepper. Arrange all the other ingredients on a serving dish, leaving the sardines till last, pour over the dressing and serve immediately.

BABY SARDINES IN OLIVE OIL WITH RADISHES AND SAUERKRAUT

* 1x 135g tin Parmentier's *petites sardines aux deux olives* (**or other sardines**)
* 2–3 radishes, washed, trimmed and sliced
* 1 tablespoon sauerkraut or kimchi from a jar
* 1 slice of bread of your choice, toasted
* a little lemon juice
* black pepper

Arrange the sauerkraut or kimchi on the toast, add the sardines then the radishes and season with the lemon juice and a good grind of black pepper.

SUPER-FAST SMOKED MACKEREL PATE

* 100g smoked mackerel fillets
* 3 spring onions
* 1 teaspoon horseradish sauce or cream
* 1 teaspoon grain or Dijon mustard
* 2 tablespoons natural yoghurt
* juice ½ lemon
* pepper

Remove the skin from the mackerel and place in a mini blender with the other ingredients, pulsing rather than fast whizzing in order to keep a little texture.

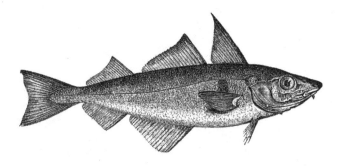

SMOKED HADDOCK KEDGEREE WITH GIANT WHOLEGRAIN WILD RICE AND ASPARAGUS

* 100g wholegrain rice
* 130g fresh or frozen smoked haddock
* milk
* 1 hard-boiled egg
* juice ½ lemon
* 1 small red onion, finely sliced
* ½ teaspoon medium curry powder
* 1 teaspoon vegetable oil
* 1 tablespoon parsley, chopped
* cayenne pepper
* 100g asparagus, sliced
* salt and freshly ground black pepper

Preheat the oven to 180°C (fan). Begin by cooking the rice according to the pack instructions and drain. Place the haddock fillet in a shallow ovenproof dish and just cover with cold milk and bake for about 8 minutes. Remove the skin (if present) and flake the fish into the rice; reserve the cooking liquid. In a small non-stick frying pan add a teaspoon of oil and the finely sliced red onion plus ½ cupful of water. Allow to cook gently for the water to evaporate. When the onion begins to take on colour stir in the curry powder, fry for a minute and add to the rice. Cook the asparagus pieces in a little boiling water for about 3 minutes. Drain and add to the rice. Return the rice, fish, etc. to a frying pan along with the parsley, salt and pepper. Moisten with a little of the milk in which the fish cooked and stir in the lemon juice. When thoroughly hot, tip into a pretty dish and scatter over the sliced hard-boiled egg, sprinkle a pinch of cayenne pepper using a fine tea strainer and serve immediately.

BAKED HADDOCK WITH TOMATOES, SPINACH AND QUARK

(GF)

* 130g haddock
* 2 tomatoes, roughly chopped
* 250g spinach, thoroughly washed
* 2–3 tablespoons quark (or cream cheese)
* 1 heaped tablespoon grated Parmesan
* 1 teaspoon olive oil
* salt and freshly ground black pepper

Preheat the oven to 180°C (fan). Steam the spinach and squeeze out as much moisture as possible and lay in a small ovenproof dish. Place the fish on top and surround with the tomatoes. Spoon on the quark or cream cheese, scatter the Parmesan and season. Finally, drizzle with the olive oil and bake for about 15 minutes (or longer, if the fish is frozen) until bubbling.

SALMON WITH PRAWNS AND VEGETABLE STIR-FRY

(DF) (GF)

* 130g salmon
* 175g North Atlantic cold-water prawns
* juice 1 lemon
* vegetable oil
* 1 leek, sliced
* 4–6 radishes, washed, trimmed and sliced
* 100g asparagus, sliced
* ½ cucumber, cut into batons
* 1 clove garlic, peeled and chopped
* soy

If cooking from frozen, place the salmon in a small non-stick frying pan with a splash of vegetable oil, season, cover and cook very gently for about 5 minutes. Turn the fish, replace the lid and cook a further 2 minutes before adding the prawns and the lemon juice. In the meantime, heat a splash of oil in a wok and add all the vegetables. Stir and cook for 3 minutes before adding the soy. Serve immediately.

SALMON WITH PUY LENTILS

DF GF

* 130g salmon (skin removed if necessary)
* juice ½ lemon
* 1 clove garlic, chopped
* 125g or ½ pouch ready-cooked Puy lentils
* sea salt and freshly ground black pepper

Preheat the oven to 180°C (fan). Place the fish in a small ovenproof dish, scatter over the garlic and lemon juice. Season and cover with foil. Bake for about 6–8 minutes. Heat the lentils according to the pack instructions and serve them with some fine French beans tossed in a little olive oil.

BAKED SALMON WITH SORREL SAUCE

GF

* 130g salmon
* juice 1 lemon
* splash olive oil
* salt and freshly ground black pepper

FOR THE SAUCE:

* 100ml white wine
* 1 small shallot, finely chopped
* 100g fresh sorrel leaves, stripped from the stalks
* 1 tablespoon crème fraîche or double cream
* 2 tablespoons water
* 1 teaspoon butter
* salt and freshly ground black pepper

Preheat the oven to 180°C (fan). Remove the skin from the salmon and place in a small ovenproof dish. Drizzle with a little olive oil and the lemon juice. Season and bake for about 5–8 minutes depending on the thickness of the fillet. To make the sauce, place the wine, shallot and 2 tablespoons of water in a small saucepan. Bring to the boil, reduce the heat and simmer until most of the liquid has evaporated. Stir in the crème fraîche/cream and butter and add the finely chopped sorrel. Simmer gently, adding a little water if necessary, for about 2 minutes to wilt the sorrel. Season and pour over the fish. Serve immediately with steamed asparagus and radishes.

SALMON AND LIME FISHCAKES

* 130g salmon, skin removed and chopped into small chunks
* ½ green or red chilli, deseeded and sliced
* small handful fresh herbs: dill, parsley and/or coriander
* 2 spring onions, sliced
* zest ½ lime
* 2 teaspoons gram flour
* salt and freshly ground black pepper

Preheat the oven to 180°C (fan). Mix everything together well and divide into two fishcakes. Allow to settle in the fridge before shallow-frying or spraying lightly with oil and baking in the oven for about 10 minutes.

BAKED SALMON WITH JERSEY ROYAL POTATO, COURGETTE, LEEK AND ASPARAGUS

For 1

* 130g salmon (either fresh or frozen)
* 1 large Jersey royal potato (130g), scrubbed and sliced
* 1 courgette, sliced
* 1 leek, sliced
* 200g asparagus, sliced
* 1 clove garlic, chopped
* olive oil
* juice ½ lemon
* splash white wine (optional)
* salt and pepper

Preheat the oven to 180°C (fan). Lay the potato slices into a shallow ovenproof dish and then add the other vegetables. Drizzle with about 1 tablespoon of olive oil, add the garlic and season. Bake for about 20 minutes or until the potato is almost cooked. Snuggle in the fish and cover with some of the vegetables. Add the lemon juice, white wine if using and season well. Return to the oven and bake until the salmon is cooked through. If using frozen fish, it will take a little longer.

MONKFISH WITH CAPERS

GF

* 130g monkfish
* vegetable oil
* 1 tablespoon capers, roughly chopped
* juice ½ lemon
* 1 teaspoon butter
* parsley, chopped

Trim away any sinewy bits from the monkfish and cut into scallop-sized pieces. Heat a little vegetable oil in a non-stick frying pan and cook the fish gently for about 3 minutes on each side. Remove and keep warm. In a clean pan, melt the butter and add the capers and lemon juice. Allow to bubble for a minute or until it turns a 'noisette' brown colour – then add the fish to reheat for a moment. Pile onto a plate and sprinkle with some chopped parsley and serve with a simple vegetable. I steamed some leeks with sliced fennel, the aniseed flavour of the latter going well with the fish.

TUNA AND QUARK FISHCAKES

* 1x 80g tin tuna, drained
* 2 tablespoons quark or cream cheese (full fat)
* 1 red onion, finely chopped
* 1 clove garlic, crushed
* 1 tablespoon mixed parsley and chives
* zest and juice ½ lemon
* 1–2 slices multi-seeded bread, made into crumbs (1 slice should be fine if the egg is small, adding a bit more if not firm enough)
* 1 egg
* 2 tablespoons gram flour
* salt and freshly ground black pepper
* 1 teaspoon oil

Heat the oil in a small non-stick pan and gently soften the onion. Put to one side to cool. In a bowl mix all the ingredients including the onion and smooth the surface of the mixture. Put into the fridge for about ½ hour to firm up. To ensure that the fishcakes are the same size divide the mixture in the bowl into quarters. Shape into cakes, cover lightly with gram flour and fry gently for about 3–4 minutes on each side. Serve with a salad, sliced avocado and/or baked tomatoes plus a lemon wedge or two.

TUNA AND PASTA BAKE

* 1x 80g tin tuna, drained
* 1x 160g tin sweetcorn
* 300g dried spiral pasta
* 1 tomato, roughly chopped
* ½ red chilli, deseeded and finely sliced
* handful flat-leafed parsley, roughly chopped
* 1 red onion, sliced
* 1 clove garlic, sliced
* juice and zest ½ lemon
* 50g feta, crumbled
* 50g pecorino, grated
* 2 heaped tablespoons crème fraîche
* salt and freshly ground black pepper
* 1 heaped tablespoon brown breadcrumbs
* olive oil

Preheat the oven to 180°C (fan). Begin by boiling water in a pan, add salt and the pasta. Heat a little olive oil in a small frying pan and add the red onion. Cook on a medium heat for 3 minutes, add the garlic, tomato and chilli and cook a further 3 minutes. When the pasta is cooked but still with a little bite, drain quickly leaving a little of the cooking water, add the onion, tomato, etc. and stir in the crème fraiche, pecorino, feta, parsley, lemon juice and zest. Check for seasoning and tip into an ovenproof dish. Top with a scattering of the brown breadcrumbs, drizzle with a little more olive oil and bake for 10–15 minutes or until bubbling and beginning to crisp on top.

BAKED TROUT

* 130g trout fillet per person
* 2 tablespoons crème fraîche
* juice 1 lemon
* 2 tablespoons Noilly Prat vermouth
* 1 tablespoon chopped parsley
* salt and pepper

Preheat oven to 180°C (fan). Cut the trout fillets in half down the middle and roll up. Place in a small ovenproof dish. Mix the other ingredients and pour over the fish. Bake for about 10 minutes until bubbling. Serve with creamy mashed potato.

HADDOCK AND SWEET POTATO FISHCAKES

GF (IF USING GLUTEN-FREE BREAD)

* 130g haddock (frozen)
* a little milk
* 2 tablespoons thawed frozen petits pois, lightly crushed
* 2 sprigs mint, chopped finely (about 1 tablespoon when chopped)
* ½ red chilli, deseeded and sliced
* zest 1 lemon
* ½ sweet potato (125g), peeled, cooked and mashed lightly
* 1 slice wholemeal bread or Vogel's soya and linseed bread made into crumbs
* salt and freshly ground black pepper

Preheat the oven to 180˚C (fan). Put the frozen haddock into a small non-stick pan and half cover with milk. Bring to the boil, reduce the heat and simmer until almost cooked. Remove, drain and allow to cool, removing skin if necessary. Cook the sweet potato until almost soft, drain and roughly mash. Put the haddock into a bowl and flake the fish. Add the sweet potato and all the other ingredients. Shape into 2 cakes, place on a plate and keep in the fridge for an hour or so. Either shallow-fry in a little vegetable or sunflower oil or spray with a low-calorie olive oil and bake on a preheated oven tray, middle shelf for about 10 minutes or until golden brown.

SIMPLE FISH PIE

* 130g haddock per person (thawed if frozen), any skin removed and cut into chunks
* 1 hard-boiled egg per person, roughly chopped
* white sauce with parsley
* juice 1 lemon
* mashed potato
* butter
* salt and pepper

Preheat the oven to 180˚C (fan). Place the fish in a gratin dish and scatter the egg on top and season with salt and pepper. Make the white sauce (see page 175) and fold in the chopped parsley and lemon juice and pour over the fish. Put the mashed potato into an icing bag fitted with a large nozzle and pipe on top of the fish. Dot with butter and bake until bubbling and golden. Serve with tomato ketchup.

BAKED COD WITH SIDE TREATS

This is a traditional way of serving fish in Denmark on Good Friday but makes a delicious meal at any time of the year.

* 240g cod
* 450g new potatoes – Jersey royals if possible – scrubbed and skins on
* 4 cooked beetroots, peeled and roughly chopped
* 2 hard-boiled eggs, roughly chopped
* 2 shallots or 1 red onion, finely chopped
* 2 large gherkins, chopped
* 1 tablespoon capers, roughly chopped
* 1 tablespoon parsley, chopped
* 1 tablespoon dill, chopped
* melted butter
* salt and freshly ground black pepper

FOR COOKING THE FISH:

* 1 onion, sliced
* 1 bay leaf
* 6 peppercorns
* a pinch salt

Preheat the oven to 180°C (fan). First cook the potatoes and keep warm. Place the fish onto a piece of aluminium foil with the onion, bay leaf, peppercorns and salt. Make a sealed parcel and bake on a baking tray for about 8–10 minutes. Place the beetroot, eggs, shallots/onion, capers, gherkins and parsley either in little heaps on a serving dish or in individual ramekins. Remove the fish from the foil and lift off any skin or bones before placing onto a warm plate. Scatter the chopped dill over the hot potatoes and serve immediately. Everyone takes a bit of everything before drizzling over the melted butter and seasoning.

PRAWN AND MELON STARTER

GF

* 150g North Atlantic cold-water prawns
* 1 ripe melon (cantaloupe or ogen)
* 4 tablespoons good-quality mayonnaise
* 2 tablespoons ketchup
* juice 1 lemon
* Tabasco sauce
* salt and pepper
* paprika
* lettuce (little gem, cos or iceberg)
* cress

If you have a melon baller, use it to extract the flesh. If not, cut the melon into small chunks. Put into a bowl and add the prawns. Decorate a serving dish with lettuce leaves. C o m b i n e thoroughly the mayonnaise, ketchup, lemon juice, 3–4 shakes of Tabasco, a little salt and lots of pepper before folding in the prawns and melon. Tip onto the lettuce and sprinkle with a little paprika and then the cress. Serve with a mountain of buttered wholemeal bread or warmed baguette and slices of lemon.

SMOKED SALMON TERRINES

GF

* 100g smoked salmon
* 150g cream cheese
* 1 tablespoon dill, chopped
* 1 tablespoon horseradish cream
* ½ cucumber, peeled and finely chopped
* ground black pepper
* paprika (optional)

Dig out your retro seventies ramekins or find a larger dish. Moisten the inside(s) with water and line with cling film making sure there is enough overlap to fold over when filled. Line each ramekin or the dish with smoked salmon slices and trim off any excess, which you can add to the cream cheese mixture later. Put said cream cheese into a bowl and beat with a fork to make it smooth. Add the dill, horseradish cream and cucumber. Season well with ground black pepper (no need for extra salt). If liked, add a pinch or two of paprika at the same time. Fill the ramekins or the dish with the mixture, pressing into the corners, and fold over the excess cling film. Store in the fridge to set and when about to serve, peel back the cling film and tip onto individual or one plate(s) and remove the cling film. Decorate with sprigs of dill and lemon wedges.

SALMON AND WATERCRESS QUICHE

* 130g salmon per person, cut into chunks
* 1 tablespoon capers, roughly chopped
* 3 spring onions, sliced
* 100g watercress, roughly chopped
* pinch chilli flakes
* zest 1 lemon
* 2 eggs
* 3 tablespoons crème fraîche
* salt and pepper

FOR THE PASTRY:

* 150g plain flour
* 25g porridge oats
* 75g butter

Preheat the oven to 180°C (fan). Begin by making the pastry: put the flour and oats into a small blender and whizz until powdery. Add the butter and whizz again till it resembles breadcrumbs. Add 1–2 tablespoons of cold water and whizz until it forms a ball. Remove the pastry and shape into a disc before wrapping in cling film. Put in the fridge for 30 minutes. Roll the pastry between two sheets of baking parchment or cling film to thicker than a £1 coin and drop it into a flan ring. Prick the bottom with a fork and lay one of the pieces of parchment on top and cover with baking beads if you have them or any dried pulses, butter beans for example, kept for the purpose. Bake in the oven for 15 minutes, remove the beads/beans and parchment and cook for a further 5 minutes. Beat the eggs with the crème fraîche and season with salt and pepper. Lay the fish, capers, spring onions, chilli flakes and chopped watercress on the pastry and pour over the egg mixture. Bake for about 25 minutes or until it is puffed up and golden. Serve warm (not hot from the oven) with tomato or green salad.

BREADED FISH

In this recipe I suggest using salmon because the combination of colours, flavours and added crunch is appealing and it is a different way from the usual method of cooking this good-value protein. You can also use either fresh or frozen (thaw first) cod or haddock fillets.

* 2x 130g salmon fillets (or cod, or haddock)
* flour for coating
* 1 beaten egg
* browned breadcrumbs (see below)
* 1 unwaxed lemon
* 50/50 oil and butter – approximately 1 tablespoon of each
* salt and pepper
* pinch dried chilli flakes

Preheat the oven to 180°C (fan). Remove the skin from the fish and any bones – run your finger along the fillet and you will find them. Find three small dishes: fill the first with flour, the second with the beaten egg, the third with the browned breadcrumbs. Wash the lemon and grate the zest into the last and mix. Keeping one hand for 'dry', the other for 'wet', dredge the fish first in the flour, then into the egg and finally into the crumbs making sure all the surface is coated. If you wish, you can place the breaded fillets in the fridge until needed. Place the fish o to a greased baking tray and season with salt and pepper and the chilli flakes. Drizzle a little oil or dot with butter and put on the middle shelf. Bake for about 8–10 minutes. Serve with mashed potato, green vegetables (for colour) and perhaps some carrots to match the salmon. Cut the lemon into wedges and serve alongside.

BROWNED BREADCRUMBS

This is a good way to use up any leftover stale bread. Preheat the oven to 180°C (fan). Tear the bread into chunks and lay on a baking tray and bake until lightly brown and crisp. Blitz to a crumb in a blender and cool before storing in an airtight jar. These will keep for a couple of weeks.

POULTRY AND GAME

Supermarkets are great hunting grounds for reduced items which, under normal circumstances, might not be included on your shopping list because of cost. Therefore, I search out organic, free-range chicken, guinea fowl, duck, etc. and once home, using strong kitchen scissors, I cut them into individual pieces which I freeze to take out as and when required.

SPATCHCOCKED BREADED CHICKEN

* 1x 1.45kg free-range (organic if possible) chicken
* 1 onion, sliced
* 1 stick celery, sliced
* 2 teaspoons dried mixed herbs
* 1 clove garlic, chopped
* ¼ teaspoon chilli flakes (optional)
* zest 1 lemon
* 2 tablespoons browned breadcrumbs (see page 139)
* olive oil
* salt and pepper

Preheat the oven to 180°C (fan). To spatchcock the chicken, using strong kitchen scissors or a knife, cut away the spine. Open out the bird and flatten by pressing down on the breast. Put the onion and celery into an ovenproof dish and place the chicken on top. Rub the skin with the herbs, salt, pepper, garlic and chilli flakes. Sprinkle over the breadcrumbs and drizzle with olive oil. Roast until the juices run clear. Drain off the fat and allow the chicken to rest for 10 minutes. Cut the chicken into 8 pieces (the breast into 4 and the legs divided in 2).

CHICKEN WITH GREEN PEPPER AND MUSHROOMS

* 1x 165g chicken breast per person
* 100g button mushrooms
* 1 green pepper
* 1 lemon
* white sauce made with milk, flour and butter (quantity depending on how many mouths. 150ml milk should make enough for two people)
* salt and pepper

Preheat the oven to 180°C (fan). Put the chicken breasts in a pan and cover with cold water. Bring to the boil and simmer for about 10 minutes until cooked. When cool enough to handle, remove any skin if necessary and cut the meat into chunks.

Make the white sauce by melting the butter with the flour and cooking for a minute before whisking in the milk to avoid lumps. Stir constantly until thick and season with salt and pepper. Pour a small quantity of the sauce into a dish for later.

Grate the zest from the lemon and put to one side then squeeze the juice.

Quickly rinse any dirt from the mushrooms and cut in half and cook in a pan with half the lemon juice and a little water. When cooked, strain any remaining juices into the larger quantity of white sauce. Keep the mushrooms warm.

Cut the green pepper in half and remove any ribs and seeds. Slice finely and cook in a teaspoon of butter until soft. Add the lemon zest and the remaining lemon juice to the white sauce. Fold in the green pepper and pour into a shallow gratin dish. Lay the chicken pieces on top and cover with the cup of white sauce you set aside. Scatter the mushrooms around the edge and bake for about 10 minutes until bubbling and hot. Serve with plain boiled rice and something green.

LEMONY CHICKEN BREASTS

* 1x 165g chicken breast with skin on per person
* juice 1 lemon
* salt and pepper
* butter

Preheat the oven to 180°C (fan). Put the chicken breast on to a flat oven dish. Squeeze over the lemon juice, season with salt and pepper and dot with butter. Bake in the oven for 20 minutes or until the juices run clear and the skin is golden and crispy. Serve with pasta and petits pois.

CHICKEN BREASTS WITH PANCETTA OR PARMA HAM

* 1x 165g chicken breast per person
* 1 tablespoon per breast of any sort of cheese you fancy or have handy, i.e. mozzarella, feta, Brie, Camembert, Stilton, dolcelatte, etc.
* 3 slices Parma ham or pancetta
* 1 clove garlic, chopped
* 1 teaspoon dried herbs, or handful of fresh, chopped
* salt and pepper
* juice 1 lemon
* 1 glass white wine

Preheat the oven to 180°C (fan). Remove any skin from the chicken. Find the opening in the fillet and fill with cheese. Wrap each breast in either the Parma ham or pancetta, tucking the ends under before placing in a gratin dish. Sprinkle the garlic and herbs over the chicken. Season cautiously with salt but lots of pepper. Pour over the lemon juice and white wine and bake for about 20 minutes or until the juices run clear, basting a couple of times during the cooking. You may need to add a drop or two of water or wine during the cooking. Serve with basmati rice and vegetables of your choice.

CHICKEN AND GREEN VEGETABLE STIR-FRY

DF GF (IF OMITTING EGG NOODLES AND USING EDAMAME NOODLES)

* 200g leftover cooked chicken, cut into pieces
* 125g asparagus spears, sliced on the diagonal
* 160g sugar snap peas, sliced on the diagonal
* 110g French beans, sliced
* 1 clove garlic, crushed
* 1 nest egg noodles per person
* soy
* vegetable oil
* toasted sesame oil

Cook the noodles according to pack instructions. Heat the vegetable oil in a wok and add the vegetables and garlic. Stir, add a splash of water and cover. Cook for 2–3 minutes and add the chicken and noodles. Splash in some soy, stir and cover again for a further 2 minutes. Remove from the heat, drizzle with the toasted sesame oil and serve immediately.

STEAMED CABBAGE PARCELS WITH CHICKEN

DF GF

* 2 large outer cabbage leaves
* 125g chicken breast, skin removed
* 2 tablespoons ready-cooked red and white quinoa
* zest 1 lemon
* ½ teaspoon dried mixed herbs
* 2 ready-to-eat dried apricots, finely chopped
* 1 clove garlic, crushed
* 1 teaspoon soy
* 1 stick celery, finely sliced
* 1 red onion, finely chopped
* salt and black pepper

Blanch the cabbage leaves for a couple of minutes in a pan of boiling water. Drain and put to one side to cool. Finely chop the chicken. Heat a little oil in a pan, add the onion and celery plus a little water, stirring until they soften and the liquid has evaporated. Stir in the chicken and garlic and lightly seal. Remove from the heat and add the herbs, apricots, lemon zest and quinoa and season lightly with salt but several grinds of black pepper. When cool enough to handle, pack into the cabbage leaves and try to close these as much as possible with cocktail sticks or cotton thread. It doesn't matter if they are a little untidy. Place in the bottom of a steamer over boiling water and splash with a touch more soy, cover with a lid and steam for about 10 minutes or until the chicken is thoroughly cooked and they are piping hot. Remove cocktail sticks and thread. Serve with another vegetable such as carrots or grilled tomatoes.

CHICKEN WITH MUSHROOMS AND LEMON

GF

* 200g chicken taken from cold roast
* 75g Portobello mushrooms, cut into small slices
* zest and juice ½ lemon
* small amount vegetable oil
* 2 tablespoons crème fraîche
* chicken stock made from carcass or 1 jelly pot

Heat a little oil in a wok and add the mushrooms. Stir, cover and cook on a medium heat for 5 minutes. Add the lemon juice, zest, chicken and enough stock to moisten. Bring to the boil and allow the chicken to warm through completely and some of the stock to evaporate. Stir in the crème fraîche and season. Serve with steamed asparagus or any other green vegetable.

BAKED CHICKEN BREAST WITH LEEK, BUTTER BEANS AND FENNEL

 DF GF

* 165g chicken breast, skin removed
* 1 fennel bulb, sliced
* 1 leek, sliced
* 1 clove garlic, crushed
* juice ½ lemon
* 1x 400g tin butter beans, drained and rinsed
* ½ teaspoon dried mixed herbs
* 2 teaspoons olive oil
* salt and pepper

Preheat the oven to 180°C (fan). Scatter the vegetables into a shallow ovenproof dish and snuggle in the chicken breast. Sprinkle with the herbs, squeeze over the lemon juice, drizzle with the olive oil and season with salt and pepper. Cover with foil and bake for 20 minutes, then remove the foil and continue cooking a further 10 minutes or until the chicken is cooked and the juices run clear.

BOILED CHICKEN WITH CABBAGE AND VEGETABLES

GF

Having previously eaten the breasts from a chicken I was left with the legs and thighs which I put into a large stewpot with one sliced leek, a stick of celery and a couple of chopped carrots. I cut a Savoy cabbage in half and then again, snuggling the two quarters in on top of everything. It was a gentle meal, perhaps not the most exciting, but fitted the bill and I am left with wonderful chicken broth for today which I shall pimp up with some wholewheat rice noodles, chilli flakes and a dash of soy.

CHICKEN CURRY

GF (CHECK CONTENT OF CURRY POWDER)

* 165g chicken breast, skin removed and cut into chunks
* 1 red onion, sliced
* 2 cloves garlic, chopped
* 3cm piece ginger, peeled and grated
* 2 tomatoes, roughly chopped
* 1 chicken jelly stock pot
* 1 tablespoon tomato purée
* 1 teaspoon medium curry powder
* 160g sugar snap peas
* 150g baby broad beans (frozen)
* 1 green chilli, deseeded and sliced
* handful fresh coriander, roughly chopped
* 2 tablespoons natural full-fat yoghurt
* 1 tablespoon vegetable or sunflower oil

Heat the oil in a wok and add the onion. Reduce the heat and cook for about 5 minutes. Add the curry powder and fry for 1 minute then add the chicken pieces. Seal the meat, continuing to stir then add the garlic, tomatoes, tomato purée, chilli and chicken stock. Stir in about 110ml of boiling water and cook on a gentle heat for 5 minutes before adding the sugar snap peas and broad beans. Bring back to the boil and simmer, stirring every now and then, until everything is cooked and some of the liquid has evaporated. Do not check for seasoning until the chicken is thoroughly cooked or you could end up with a sore tummy. Remove from the heat and allow to cool slightly before gradually stirring in the yoghurt, which shouldn't curdle. Sprinkle with chopped fresh coriander and serve with mango chutney and a simple dhal of red lentils, cooked according to the pack instructions.

LEFTOVER CHICKEN CURRY WITH APPLE

  (CHECK CONTENT OF CURRY POWDER)

* 200g cooked chicken (skin removed) picked from the carcass
* 570ml stock made from the bones with celery, onion and carrot, strained and degreased
* 1 large, ripe beef tomato or 3 medium tomatoes, roughly chopped
* 1 red onion, sliced
* 1 clove garlic, sliced
* 1 tablespoon concentrated tomato purée
* 1 heaped teaspoon medium curry powder
* 1 apple, peeled and roughly chopped
* vegetable oil

Heat a wok and add a splash (1 tablespoon) of oil. Add the onion, stir and pour in a good cup of water. Bring to the boil and reduce the heat to medium. The onion will cook gently, with the occasional stir and, once the water has evaporated, add the curry powder and fry for a minute or so. Add the tomatoes, apple, garlic, tomato purée and chilli and cook for 2–3 minutes before adding the stock and chicken pieces. Bring to the boil, cover and reduce the heat allowing it to simmer until the vegetables are cooked and the juices reduced slightly. Check for seasoning before serving with plain basmati rice and an accompaniment such as cucumber raita (see page 82) or a simple side dish of chopped tomato, onion and fresh coriander.

ALL-IN-ONE CHICKEN STEW

* 4 chicken thighs, skin on
* 1 leek, sliced
* 200g Jersey royal potatoes, scrubbed and roughly chopped
* 8 cherry tomatoes, halved
* 1 red pepper, deseeded and roughly chopped
* 1 chicken/vegetable jelly pot/stock cube
* 1 tablespoon concentrated tomato purée
* zest and juice 1 lemon
* 2 cloves garlic, sliced
* bouquet garni of fresh herbs: rosemary, thyme, parsley
* 1 red onion, sliced
* vegetable or sunflower oil
* salt and freshly ground pepper

Heat a tablespoon of oil in a deep pan or wok and brown the chicken pieces on a medium heat for about 6 minutes. Turn them over and add the other ingredients. Stir for a couple of minutes and add about 275ml of water. Do not season – or taste – at this point as the chicken is still raw in the middle. Cover and simmer for a further 20 minutes, checking now and then to see if more water should be added. Before serving, remove the chicken skin and discard.

CHICKEN CURRY WITH RED LENTILS

DF **GF** (CHECK CONTENT OF CURRY POWDER)

* 165g chicken breast (skinless), cut into chunks
* 1 onion, sliced
* 1 clove garlic, sliced
* 3cm root ginger, peeled and finely grated
* 275ml chicken stock
* 1 large tomato, roughly chopped
* 1 tablespoon tomato purée
* 1 tablespoon sultanas
* 2 teaspoons mild curry powder
* 1 dessertspoon sunflower oil
* small handful fresh coriander, roughly chopped
* 100g red lentils, cooked separately according to pack instructions

Put the onion, garlic and ginger in a small food processor or blender and blitz to a purée. Heat the sunflower oil in a pan and gently cook the onion/ginger/garlic mix for about 1 minute, stirring to prevent burning. Add the curry powder and stir for a minute before adding the chicken and cook a further 3 minutes. Add the tomato, tomato purée, stock and sultanas, bring to the boil, stir, cover and simmer gently for about 15–20 minutes. Thoroughly wash the lentils and put into a pan with 4 times the amount of water. Bring to the boil and cook rapidly for 5 minutes, stirring once in a while. Reduce the heat, cover and simmer, checking and stirring (you may have to add a little more water), until the water has mostly evaporated and the lentils are soft. Season with salt to taste. Scatter the coriander leaves over the curry and serve with the lentils and mango chutney.

PARTRIDGE BREASTS WITH A PEAR POACHED IN LEMON JUICE AND WATER, MASHED SWEET POTATO WITH CARROT AND STEAMED KALETTES, SCATTERED WITH BASIL

* 2 skinless partridge breasts (80g)
* 1 pear, peeled and cut into small chunks
* 2 carrots, roughly chopped
* juice ½ lemon
* 1 organic sweet potato (240g), peeled and roughly chopped
* 1 tablespoon olive oil
* 200g kalettes
* fresh sweet basil leaves
* salt and freshly ground black pepper

Gently poach the pear in the lemon juice and a little water. Cook the sweet potato and carrots in salted water, drain and mash adding plenty of freshly ground black pepper. Heat the olive oil in a non-stick pan and slowly fry the partridge breasts, turning once, adding the pears for the last minute so they take on the juices in the pan and a little colour. Season with salt and freshly ground black pepper. Steam the kalettes and pack into a crumpet ring with the mash on top. Carefully lift off and serve alongside the partridge breasts and pear. Strew with torn sweet basil leaves. 'Cheffy' but fun!

TURKEY AND COURGETTE BURGER

* 150g turkey breast, cut into chunks and quickly blitzed
* 1 courgette, spiralised or grated
* zest ½ lemon
* ½ teaspoon smoked paprika
* ½ green chilli, deseeded and chopped
* several sprigs fresh mint, roughly chopped
* salt and pepper

Preheat the oven to 180°C (fan). Mix all together and shape into a burger. Rest in the fridge for at least an hour and either fry in a little oil or bake for about 30 minutes or until the turkey is thoroughly cooked.

FAT-FREE TURKEY AND VEGETABLE CURRY WITH CHICKPEAS

  (CHECK CONTENT OF CURRY POWDER)

* 150g turkey breast, cut into chunks
* 1 onion, finely sliced
* 1x 400g tin chickpeas, drained and rinsed
* 1x 400g tin cherry tomatoes
* ½ each red and yellow pepper, deseeded and roughly chopped
* ½ aubergine (150g), sliced
* 1–2 cloves garlic, crushed
* 3cm fresh root ginger, peeled and finely cut into small pieces
* 1 heaped teaspoon medium curry powder
* 500ml chicken stock
* 200g spinach
* salt and pepper
* fresh coriander

Put the onion in a pan or wok with a little water and cook until the onion is soft and the water evaporated. Add the turkey and seal for a minute or so, stirring so it doesn't stick. Add everything else except the spinach and coriander, mix well and bring to the boil. Cover and simmer for about 10–15 minutes stirring every now and again. Finally, add the well-washed spinach and cook for a further minute or so. Sprinkle with fresh chopped coriander and serve.

TURKEY BREAST ESCALOPE WITH CHILLI, LEMON ZEST AND GARLIC

DF GF

* 150g turkey breast, beaten with a rolling pin between a piece of cling film
* 1 tablespoon gram flour
* zest ½ lemon
* ½ chilli, deseeded and finely sliced
* 1 clove garlic, chopped
* salt and freshly ground black pepper
* a little vegetable oil for frying

Mix the gram flour, chilli, lemon zest and garlic in a small dish and season with salt and freshly ground black pepper. Cover the turkey escalope with the mixture, heat a very little oil in a non-stick pan and cook gently on each side for about 3 minutes, or until the juices run clear. Serve with a green salad or vegetable of your choice and with a couple of lemon wedges.

TURKEY, AUBERGINE AND PEPPER CURRY

  (CHECK CONTENT OF CURRY POWDER)

* 220g turkey breast, cut into chunks
* ½ aubergine (150g), roughly chopped
* ½ red pepper, deseeded and roughly chopped
* ½ green or yellow pepper, deseeded and roughly chopped
* 1 red onion, sliced
* 3–4 tomatoes, roughly chopped
* 1 tablespoon concentrated tomato purée
* 1 chicken jelly stock pot
* small handful fresh coriander, roughly chopped
* 1–2 cloves garlic, chopped
* 1 heaped teaspoon medium curry powder
* 1 tablespoon vegetable or sunflower oil
* Salt and pepper

Put the onion in a wok with the oil and about 2 tablespoons of water. Bring to the boil, stir and simmer until the liquid has evaporated and the onion is soft and taking on a little colour. Add the turkey, stir and cook for 2–3 minutes before adding all the other ingredients except the coriander. Stir in about 275ml of water, bring to the boil and simmer for about 15–20 minutes until thoroughly cooked and the liquid has reduced. Only now check for seasoning and adjust accordingly. When ready to serve, sprinkle with roughly chopped coriander and serve with a vegetable of your choice and/or lentil dhal.

PAN-FRIED TURKEY ESCALOPE AND BROAD BEANS A LA CREME

* 150g turkey breast per person
* 1 tablespoon gram flour
* zest ½ lemon
* 2 teaspoons grated Parmesan
* salt and freshly ground pepper
* little oil for frying
* 150g broad beans (fresh or frozen)
* parsley
* dill weed
* 1 tablespoon crème fraîche

Place the turkey breast between a piece of cling film and beat flat with a rolling pin. Mix the gram flour, lemon zest and Parmesan and cover the turkey escalope, pressing it so that it sticks. Heat a little oil in a small non-stick pan and add the turkey, cooking gently for about 2–3 minutes. Turn and cook a further 2–3 minutes until crispy and golden and the juices run clear. In the meantime, cook the podded broad beans in a little salted water for about 3 minutes, drain and run under the cold tap. Squeeze out the green beans from the skin (which you discard) and heat in the pan with the crème fraîche and chopped herbs. Season and serve with the turkey and the rest of the lemon, cut in wedges.

GUINEA FOWL CASSEROLE

* 1x 1kg guinea fowl (free-range if possible)
* 250g Portobello mushrooms, peeled and sliced
* 4 banana shallots, quartered
* 275ml red wine
* 275ml chicken/vegetable jelly stock pot
* 3 bay leaves
* salt and freshly ground black pepper
* little vegetable oil

Preheat the oven to 180°C (fan). Heat a tablespoon of vegetable oil in an ovenproof casserole and brown the guinea fowl on all sides on a medium heat. Add the shallots, mushrooms and bay leaves and stir. Cook for 5 minutes then add the stock, red wine and seasoning.* Cover and either bring to the boil on the stove, reduce the heat and cook very gently for about 50 minutes or cook in the oven until the juices run clear.

*Note: remember that jelly pots contain salt.

GUINEA FOWL WITH VEGETABLES

* 1x 1kg guinea fowl (free-range if possible)
* 2 turnips, peeled and roughly chopped
* 2 leeks, roughly chopped
* 1 large carrot, sliced
* 1 stick celery, sliced
* 2 cloves garlic, sliced
* ½ aubergine (150g), sliced
* 1 tablespoon concentrated tomato purée
* 3 bay leaves
* 1 chicken/vegetable jelly stock pot

Ease off the skin from the guinea fowl, cutting where necessary to make it easier and discard. You will probably not be able to remove it from the winglets but it will add to the flavour. Using kitchen scissors or poultry shears, cut away the back bone and discard. Open up the bird and place in a cast iron casserole surrounding it with the vegetables. Add the bay leaves, chicken/vegetable stock and about 500ml of water. Cover, bring to the boil and simmer gently for about 40 minutes or until the guinea fowl is cooked through and the meat tender.

CASSEROLE OF GUINEA FOWL WITH GREEN LENTILS

* 1x 1kg guinea fowl (free-range if possible)
* 1 leek, roughly chopped
* 2 onions, sliced
* 1 stick celery, chopped
* 150ml red wine
* 425ml chicken stock
* 1 teaspoon olive oil
* 2 teaspoons concentrated tomato purée
* salt and freshly ground black pepper
* green lentils cooked to pack instructions (or 1x 450g tin)

Preheat the oven to 180°C (fan). Heat a heavy-bottomed casserole, add the olive oil and brown the guinea fowl on all sides. Add the vegetables, stir and cook for 5 minutes before adding the wine, stock and tomato purée. Stir, cover, bring to the boil and simmer gently on the stove or cook the oven for about ¾ hour or until the juices run clear. Check for seasoning (the stock will probably already be salted) and adjust accordingly. Serve with the lentils and a vegetable of your choice, if required.

STIR-FRIED DUCK BREAST STEAK

* 175g stir-fry duck breast slices – these are different from whole duck breasts
* 100g sugar snap peas, sliced
* 100g purple sprouting broccoli, sliced
* 1 stick celery, sliced
* 175g pointed cabbage, sliced
* 1 clove garlic, chopped
* 1 tablespoon vegetable or sunflower oil
* soy

Marinate the duck with the garlic and a little soy. Heat the wok and add the oil. Add the duck meat with the marinade, stir and tip in all the vegetables. Stir, cover and cook for about 5 minutes, stirring every now and again. Serve immediately, with extra soy if needed.

PAN-FRIED PARTRIDGE BREAST WITH MUSHROOMS AND CHERRY TOMATOES

* 1x 40g partridge breast
* 6 cherry tomatoes, cut in half
* 1 red onion, chopped (or small banana shallot)
* 80g chestnut mushrooms, sliced
* 1 clove garlic, chopped
* vegetable or sunflower oil
* salt and pepper

Heat a small frying pan and add the oil, onion and mushrooms, and a splash of water. Stir, cover and cook on medium heat for 3 minutes before adding the partridge and tomatoes. Season with salt and pepper, add the garlic and a little more water. Stir and cook for about 8 minutes.

ROASTED CHICKEN CROWN WITH FENNEL AND AUBERGINE

* 1x 350g chicken crown
* 1 fennel bulb, cut in half or in quarters
* ½ aubergine (150g), cut in half

MAKE A MARINADE WITH:

* 2 tablespoons runny honey
* 2 tablespoons soy
* juice 1 lemon
* 1 tablespoon olive oil
* 2 cloves garlic, crushed

Preheat the oven to 180°C (fan). Rub the marinade into the chicken crown and leave in the fridge for about an hour before placing in a roasting dish along with the fennel and aubergine. Roast for about 40 minutes or until the juices run clear.

GUINEA FOWL BREAST WITH MUSHROOMS AND SHALLOT

* 1x 200g guinea fowl breast with winglet*
* 1 banana shallot, sliced
* 1 stick celery, sliced
* 100g chestnut mushrooms, sliced
* 1 clove garlic, sliced
* 100ml red wine
* 1 vegetable jelly stock pot
* few sprigs fresh thyme
* 1 teaspoon concentrated tomato purée
* pepper
* vegetable or sunflower oil

Heat a little oil in a wok and brown the guinea fowl breast on both sides. Remove and add the shallot, mushrooms and garlic into the pan. Stir for a minute or two, then return the guinea fowl and add the red wine, thyme, vegetable stock, tomato purée and a little water. Season with pepper, stir, cover with a lid and simmer very gently for about 20 minutes or until the juices run clear. Check the seasoning.

* Cut from a whole bird – freeze the rest for another day.

CHICKEN, MUSHROOM AND AUBERGINE CASSEROLE

* 500g skinless chicken thighs
* 1 aubergine (300g), cut into small cubes
* 150g chestnut mushrooms, sliced
* 2 banana shallots, quartered
* 1 stick celery, sliced
* 2 bay leaves
* 1 tablespoon concentrated tomato purée
* 570ml chicken stock
* 1 tablespoon vegetable or sunflower oil

Preheat the oven to 180°C (fan). Brown the chicken in the oil on both sides in an ovenproof casserole and remove. In the same pan, sweat the shallots for a few minutes or until they begin to take on a bit of colour. Add the mushrooms and celery and return the chicken to the pan with the bay leaves, aubergine and stock. Cook in the oven for about 30 minutes, or until the chicken juices run clear.

QUAIL SALAD

* 1 quail, spatchcocked* and roasted
* 100g mixed salad leaves including rocket
* small handful parsley and chives
* 6–8 cherry tomatoes, quartered
* 1 tablespoon olive oil
* 1 tablespoon cider vinegar
* 1 egg, hard-boiled and sliced
* salt and pepper

Remove the cooked meat from the quail. Mix with the salad ingredients and lay the sliced hard-boiled egg on top. Dress with olive oil, cider vinegar, salt and pepper.

* To spatchcock a bird, using scissors or a sharp knife, cut along the spine on both sides, remove and discard, then flatten the bird by pressing down on the breast bone.

CHICKEN BREAST WITH PEANUT BUTTER CRUST

* 1x 165g organic, free-range chicken breast, skin removed
* 1 tablespoon crunchy peanut butter
* juice 1 lime
* 1 clove garlic, crushed
* dash white wine
* salt and pepper

Preheat the oven to 180°C (fan). Mix together the peanut butter, garlic and lime juice and spread on the chicken breast. Place in a small ovenproof dish and add the white wine and seasoning. Bake for about 15 minutes or until the juices run clear. Serve with petits pois braised with spring onions and little gem lettuce (recipe page 72, petits pois à la française).

TURKEY AND VEGETABLE CURRY

  (CHECK CONTENT OF CURRY POWDER)

* 300g turkey breast, cut into smallish chunks
* ½ aubergine (150g), sliced and roughly chopped
* 4 tomatoes, roughly chopped
* 1 red onion, finely sliced
* ½ green pepper, deseeded and roughly chopped
* 1 tablespoon concentrated tomato purée
* 275ml chicken/vegetable stock
* 1 clove garlic, chopped
* 1 teaspoon medium curry powder
* small handful fresh coriander, roughly chopped
* salt and freshly ground black pepper
* 1 tablespoon vegetable oil

Put the oil in a wok and heat. Add the turkey, stir and cook quickly for about 2 minutes. Remove and put to one side. Add the onion to the wok plus the curry powder and stir. Cook for a minute before adding the other vegetables and the turkey. Pour in the stock but do not season – nor taste – at this point: the turkey is still raw. Bring to the boil, reduce the heat and allow to simmer for about 10 minutes or until the turkey is thoroughly cooked. Now you can check the seasoning and adjust accordingly; if using a stock cube remember that this already contains salt. Stir in the fresh chopped coriander and serve with a lentil dhal and/or plain basmati rice, a spoonful of yoghurt and some mango chutney. (Recipe page 94, Red and Yellow Dhal, omitting the yellow lentils.)

BALLOTINE OF CHICKEN WITH MUSHROOMS, SHALLOT AND PISTACHIOS

GF

* 1x 165g skinless chicken breast
* 1 banana shallot, finely chopped
* 60g chestnut mushrooms, chopped
* 1 clove garlic, chopped
* 1 tablespoon unsalted pistachios, chopped in a small blender
* 1 teaspoon dried mixed herbs
* zest and juice ½ lemon
* vegetable or olive oil
* salt and freshly ground black pepper

FOR THE SAUCE:

* 8 tarragon leaves, roughly chopped
* 1 tablespoon Greek basil, roughly chopped
* 1 heaped tablespoon crème fraîche
* salt and freshly ground black pepper

Take a piece of cling film, lay on the chicken breast, fold over the cling film and beat with a rolling pin to flatten it, reducing it to about 1cm thick. Heat the oil in a small non-stick pan and sweat the shallot for a minute, then add the mushrooms and garlic. Cook for a further 2 minutes, remove from the heat and add the lemon zest, juice, crushed pistachios, herbs and seasoning and allow to cool. Spread the filling onto the chicken breast and, using the cling film, roll it up tightly into a sausage, twisting and securing the ends by folding them under. Note: the larger the piece of chicken, the easier it will be to roll up – this piece was small and the stuffing fell out during cooking, but it tasted delicious nonetheless. Keep in the fridge until ready to cook.

Place the chicken ballotine in a pan and cover with boiling water. Simmer for about 15 minutes or until cooked (larger chicken breasts will take longer), remove from the pan and allow to rest for 5 minutes, still in the cling film. In the same pan that you sweated the shallot in, add a teaspoon of oil, unwrap the chicken and brown gently on all sides. You don't need to cook it any further, but simply give it a little colour. Remove and keep warm while you make the sauce. Add the crème fraîche to the same pan you browned the chicken in and stir, mixing in the juices, then add the basil and tarragon. You may need to slacken the sauce a little with a dash of water at this stage, then season. Slice the chicken into good 1cm slices and pour over the sauce. Serve with a vegetable of your choice or salad.

GUINEA FOWL BREAST WITH EMMER WHEAT

* 1x 200g skinless guinea fowl breast
* 80g emmer wheat, cooked according to pack instructions
* 6 baby carrots, cut on the diagonal
* 1 banana shallot, sliced
* 1 leek, sliced
* 1 clove garlic, chopped
* 1 teaspoon olive oil
* 200ml wine, water or stock
* Salt and pepper

Heat the oil in a wok and add the shallot and carrots. Stir and cook for 3 minutes. Add the guinea fowl and seal on both sides. Add the garlic, stock/wine/water and sliced leek. Stir, season and cover. Cook for about 10 minutes or until the vegetables are almost soft. I served it with emmer wheat 'farro' which was a nice, nutty accompaniment and high in fibre.

GUINEA FOWL BREAST WITH APPLE AND NOILLY PRAT

* 60ml Noilly Prat (or French vermouth)
* 2 guinea fowl breasts (400g cut from a whole bird – freeze the rest)
* 1 small red onion, sliced
* 1 dessert apple, sliced
* olive oil
* salt and pepper

Preheat the oven to 180°C (fan). Heat a little olive oil in a small frying pan and cook the guinea fowl breast skin-side down on a medium heat for 3 minutes. Turn and cook for a further minute. Remove from the pan and put to one side. Add the onion to the pan with the guinea fowl juices and cook for a minute or two, stirring to prevent burning. Add the apple slices, stir, and return the guinea fowl breast to the pan. Add the Noilly Prat, season, cover with a lid and cook for about 10 minutes or until the juices run clear. Allow to rest for 5 minutes before serving with creamed mashed potato and buttered cabbage or kale.

GUINEA FOWL BREAST WITH MUSHROOMS AND BACON

* 2 guinea fowl breasts (400g)
* 100g chestnut mushrooms, roughly chopped
* 1 red onion, sliced
* 2 rashers smoked back bacon (or 4 slices of streaky), roughly chopped
* 275ml chicken stock
* ½ teaspoon dried mixed herbs
* 2 garlic cloves, chopped
* 1 dessertspoon concentrated tomato purée
* 1 tablespoon sunflower or vegetable oil
* salt and pepper

Heat a little oil in a pan and brown the breasts, skin-side down, for 3 minutes. Put to one side. In the same pan cook the bacon with the onions for about 5 minutes. Return the breasts to the pan along with the other ingredients. Stir in the stock, bring to the boil and cover, simmering gently, stirring every now and then, for about 10 minutes or until the meat is thoroughly cooked. You may have to add a little more stock or water during the cooking. Serve with creamy, buttery mashed potatoes.

SPATCHCOCKED POUSSIN WITH ROASTED VEGETABLES

* 1 poussin (this easily feeds 2 people)
* 2 courgettes
* 2 large red salad onions, halved
* 2 large white salad onions, halved
* 1 teaspoon dried mixed Italian herbs
* olive oil
* salt and freshly ground black pepper

Preheat the oven to 180°C (fan). Remove the back bone of the poussin using sharp kitchen scissors and discard. Turn the bird over and flatten with your hand. Place in a shallow roasting tray and surround it with the courgettes cut into chunks and the halved onions. Season well, drizzle with olive oil and sprinkle a teaspoon of the dried Italian herbs. Roast for about 30–40 minutes or until the juices run clear. To be extra healthy, remove the skin and serve with another vegetable of your choice.

BRAISED DUCK LEG WITH BABY TURNIPS

* 1 duck leg per person
* 2 baby turnips per person, trimmed and roughly chopped
* 1 shallot, chopped
* 1 clove garlic, chopped
* 425ml chicken stock
* 150ml red wine
* salt and pepper

Starting with a cold pan, brown the duck legs with no added oil on a medium heat for about 5–8 minutes. Remove and put to one side. Sweat the shallot for 5 minutes and add the turnips. Cook for 2 minutes, return the duck skin-side up, add the wine and stock and garlic. Bring to the boil, reduce the heat, cover and simmer gently for about 15 minutes then remove the lid and continue cooking to allow some of the liquid to evaporate. After a further 15 minutes check for seasoning and serve with a purée of mashed sweet potato and carrot and something green.

ROAST DUCKLING WITH BAKED APPLES

* 1 fresh duckling, giblets removed
* 1 stick celery, roughly chopped
* 1 onion, chopped
* salt and pepper

Preheat the oven to 180°C (fan). Prick the skin of the duckling and place on a rack over a bowl in the sink and carefully pour over a kettle of boiling water. This will loosen the fat and make the skin extra crispy. Lay the onion and celery in the base of a large roasting dish, place the rack on top and then the duckling. Season well with salt and pepper and roast in a hot oven for about 1½ hours or until the juices run clear.

BAKED APPLES

* 1 eating apple per person
* zest and juice 1 orange
* a little butter

With an apple corer, remove the centre of the apple then with a pointed knife cut a ring around the apple just below the top – this will prevent it from bursting during cooking. Put a pinch or two of the orange zest in the hollow, topping with a knob of butter. Pour over the orange juice, adding a little water, then after the duck has been cooking for an hour, bake for about 20 minutes, or until the apples are soft. Remove the duck, place on a serving dish and cover lightly with foil. Keep the apples warm the same way.

To make the gravy, drain off the duck fat (keep it for roasting potatoes) and scrape the juices on the bottom of the roasting dish before adding about 250ml boiling water. Put back into the oven for 10 minutes and then strain into a small jug. Serve with roast potatoes and vegetables of your choice.

MEAT

Although I have cut back eating red meat I do believe it is important to include it in your diet in moderation. Also, I am not a believer in taking supplements since you find all you need to keep healthy in vegetables, fruit and other fresh foods. This is a simple way of stretching a small piece of lamb to feed two people comfortably.

LAMB AND CANNELLINI BEAN STEW

DF GF

* 250g lamb (fillet, shoulder, whatever you wish)
* 1 red onion, finely chopped
* 1x 400g tin cannellini (or haricot) beans, drained and rinsed
* 1 large ripe beef tomato or 3 medium tomatoes
* 2 bay leaves
* sprig rosemary
* 4 sprigs fresh thyme
* 1 tablespoon concentrated tomato purée
* 1 clove garlic, chopped
* 1 tablespoon oil (vegetable or sunflower)
* salt and freshly ground black pepper

Trim the lamb of fat or sinew and cut into smallish cubes. Heat a tablespoon of oil in a shallow saucepan and add the lamb, cooking quickly to seal and brown slightly. Remove from the heat and keep to one side. Add the beans and onion to the same pan. Stir and sweat for 5 minutes before adding the herbs and tomatoes. Add enough water to almost cover the vegetables and bring to a boil. Next add the tomato purée and garlic, adjust the water and bring back to a boil, cover and reduce the heat. Add the lamb and simmer gently until the meat is very tender – perhaps a further 30 minutes. Season well with salt and freshly ground black pepper and sprinkle with chopped leaf parsley.

MARINATED VENISON LOIN

* 250g venison haunch steak
* soy
* Worcestershire sauce
* 1 clove garlic, crushed

Preheat the oven to 180°C (fan). Mix all the ingredients and allow to marinate for an hour or so. Heat a non-stick pan and brown the meat on all sides, then place onto a small ovenproof dish along with the marinade juices and bake for about 10 minutes, depending on how rare you like your meat. Allow to rest for about 5 minutes before slicing.

Serve with steamed sugar snap peas, sprouting broccoli and asparagus. I fell asleep before pudding.

CABBAGE PARCELS WITH PORK AND EMMER WHEAT

* 1–2 outer leaves from a savoy cabbage per person
* 2x 3cm slices pork tenderloin per person, finely chopped
* 100g easy-cook emmer grains or any other wholegrain you choose, cooked according to pack instructions
* 100g chestnut mushrooms, finely chopped
* 1 red onion, finely chopped
* 1 tablespoon chopped parsley
* few sprigs fresh thyme, leaves only
* 1 egg, beaten
* 1 teaspoon vegetable or sunflower oil
* salt and freshly ground black pepper
* wooden cocktail sticks

Put the cabbage leaves in a saucepan and cover with boiling water. Cook for 2–3 minutes until wilted, drain and refresh under cold water. In a small pan, add the oil and the onion. Fry for 2 minutes before adding the chopped pork. Stir and lightly brown. Add the mushrooms and herbs. Remove from the heat and stir in the beaten egg and seasoning. Carefully spoon the mixture onto the cabbage leaves, folding them over lengthwise and securing with a cocktail stick. Fold in each end and secure the same way. Place the bundles into a steamer, secured side upwards and steam for about 20 minutes. Serve with a fresh tomato sauce or baked sliced tomatoes.

CORNISH PASTIES

* 1 pack ready rolled, all-butter flaky pastry
* 200g skirt (lean cut of beef) cut up into very small pieces – don't be tempted to put in blender
* 1 onion, finely chopped
* 1 potato, peeled and cut into very small pieces
* 1 egg, beaten
* salt and pepper

Preheat the oven to 180°C (fan). Place the pastry between 2 sheets of baking parchment and roll out further to the thickness of a pound coin. Using a saucer cut as many rounds as you can. Any leftover pastry can be given to the birds – they love it. In the centre of each pastry disc place the meat, potato and onion in equal quantities. Season with salt and lots of pepper. Brush one half of the pastry with some of the beaten egg and gather the edges together. I can't crimp so leave the pasties sitting upright rather like dinosaurs. Brush with more egg, place on a metal tray and bake for about 35 minutes or until the pastry is cooked and golden.

BEEF AND VEGETABLE STIR-FRY

* 200g beef (skirt, sirloin, fillet, rump), any fat trimmed and cut into slices about pound coin thickness
* vegetables of your choice. I used:
* 1 leek, finely sliced
* 1 kohlrabi, peeled and cut into sticks (or 100g cabbage of your choice, or baby turnip)
* 1 sweet red pepper, deseeded and sliced
* 2 carrots, cut into sticks
* 150g spinach
* 1 clove garlic, chopped
* 3cm piece root ginger, peeled and grated
* 1 small chilli of your choice, deseeded and chopped finely
* soy
* vegetable or sunflower oil

Heat a teaspoon of oil in a wok and add the beef slices, stirring all the while. Cook for 2 minutes, tip into a dish and put to one side. Heat another teaspoon of oil and add the kohlrabi, chilli, sweet pepper and carrots, stir and cook for 2 minutes. Tip in the spinach, garlic, leek and beef and bring up to a good heat before adding several dashes of soy. Cook for a couple more minutes and serve immediately.

LAMB SPARE RIBS

  (CHECK SAUCES FOR GLUTEN)

* 150g lamb spare ribs (per person)
* 1 onion, sliced
* 4 tablespoons tomato ketchup
* 1 tablespoon sweet chilli sauce
* 1 dessertspoon demerara sugar
* 2 cloves garlic, chopped
* juice 1 lemon
* 2 tablespoons soy
* 2 tablespoons white/red wine or cider vinegar

Preheat the oven to 180°C (fan). Mix the sauce ingredients together and then add the lamb, covering it well. Bake in an ovenproof dish for about 30–40 minutes, basting and turning the ribs every now and again. The sauce will be deliciously gooey. Drain off any fat and serve with a steaming bowl of new potatoes and a green salad.

Substitute pork for lamb ribs.

FILLET OF PORK WITH CREAMED APPLES

* 1x 400g free-range pork tenderloin, cut into medallions about 1cm thick
* 1 tablespoon vegetable or sunflower oil
* 1 onion, peeled and sliced
* 1 eating apple, cored and sliced
* 3 sage leaves, chopped
* 150ml dry cider (or white wine)
* 1 tablespoon crème fraîche or double cream
* salt and pepper

Heat the oil in a frying pan and cook the onion until it is beginning to caramelise. Put to one side. Heat the pan again and add the pork medallions turning after a minute or so. Add the cooked onion, sliced apple and sage leaves. Pour in the cider (wine) and season with salt and pepper. Stir, cover and simmer gently for about 10 minutes or until the apple is soft. Add the crème fraîche or double cream. Pasta or mashed potato go well with this.

GRATIN OF ENDIVE AND SMOKED HAM

* 1 endive per person
* 2 slices smoked ham off the bone per endive
* 1 heaped tablespoon fresh brown breadcrumbs

FOR THE CHEESE SAUCE:

* 80g grated Emmental or Gruyère cheese
* 1 tablespoon gram flour
* 1 tablespoon butter
* 1 teaspoon Dijon mustard
* 1 dessertspoon crème fraîche
* 150ml milk
* freshly grated nutmeg
* salt and pepper

Preheat the oven to 180°C (fan). Trim and cut the endive in half lengthways and put into a shallow saucepan with a sprinkle of salt. Cover with boiling water and cook until nearly soft – about 6–8 minutes. Drain thoroughly and lay side by side in a shallow ovenproof dish. When cool, wrap a slice of ham around each piece of endive and pour over the cheese sauce. Sprinkle with the brown breadcrumbs and a little extra grated cheese. Bake until brown and bubbling. Serve on its own or with a simple green salad.

For the cheese sauce: put the gram flour and butter into a non-stick saucepan, melt and whisk for a minute before adding the milk very gradually, whisking to prevent lumps. Bring to the boil, whisking all the while, remove from the heat and add the grated cheese, crème fraîche, mustard and several gratings of nutmeg. Stir and taste before seasoning with salt and pepper.

SAUCES

NO-FUSS TOMATO SAUCE

* 1x 400g tin chopped tomatoes or 450g ripe tomatoes, roughly chopped
* 2 cloves garlic, chopped
* 3 tablespoons olive oil
* salt and pepper
* ¼ teaspoon sugar

Place all the ingredients in a pan and stir. Bring to the boil, reduce the heat and let it bubble away gently, stirring frequently until it becomes almost the consistency of jam. Serve with pasta or spread on a fresh pizza base.

THE SIMPLEST OF SAUCES TO GO WITH FISH

 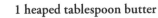

* 1 heaped tablespoon butter
* juice 1 lemon
* pinch cayenne pepper

Melt the butter gently in a pan, remove from the heat and stir in the lemon juice and cayenne. Serve hot with steamed or fried fish.

QUICK BARBECUE DIPPING SAUCE

* 1 tablespoon demerara sugar
* 4 tablespoons tomato ketchup
* 2 tablespoons soy

Put all ingredients in a small pan and bring to the heat, stirring until the sugar has dissolved. Pour into a bowl and allow to cool.

EASY-PEASY PESTO

* 2 tablespoons pine nuts
* handful fresh basil
* 1 clove garlic, chopped
* 60ml olive oil
* ¼ teaspoon dried chilli flakes (optional)
* 2 tablespoons freshly grated Parmesan
* salt and pepper to taste

Put all ingredients into a small blender and blitz but keeping a little texture. It's ready to use straight away. If not, store in the fridge in a clean jar, pouring a small amount of olive oil over the pesto before sealing.

BROCCOLI PESTO

* 80g broccoli, cut into florets
* 1 tablespoon pine nuts
* 1 clove garlic, chopped
* 2 tablespoons freshly grated Parmesan
* 60ml olive oil
* salt and pepper to taste

Steam the broccoli florets for about 5 minutes. Remove and when cool, place in a blender with the garlic, Parmesan, pine nuts and olive oil. Blitz but leaving a little texture. Season with salt and pepper to taste.

SIMPLE APPLE SAUCE

* 2 large cooking apples, peeled, cored and roughly chopped
* 1 tablespoon butter
* 1 tablespoon sugar
* 4 tablespoons water

Place all the ingredients in a pan. Bring to the boil, then simmer until soft. Mash with a fork and serve in a little bowl. This freezes well.

BAKED APPLES AS AN ACCOMPANIMENT

For 4

* 4 eating apples, cored
* 1 tablespoon sultanas or raisins
* 2 tablespoons Calvados or brandy
* 1 dessertspoon butter
* 1 tablespoon demerara sugar

Preheat the oven to 180°C (fan). Soak the dried fruit in the brandy for 1 hour. Cut a ring around each apple, ⅓ from the top – this will prevent it bursting during cooking. Spoon the soaked fruit into the cavity of each apple, top with a little butter, sprinkle with the sugar and place them in a small ovenproof dish. Bake for about 30 minutes until the apple is soft and fluffy. A perfect side dish to pheasant or roast pork.

FISHY DIP FOR CRUDITES

* 1x 60g jar anchovies in olive oil, drained
* 165g cream cheese
* 150ml single cream
* a little cold milk
* freshly ground black pepper

Drain the anchovies and place in a dish with a little cold milk. Leave for about 30 minutes, then drain, pat dry on kitchen paper and chop finely. Beat the cream cheese with the cream until light and fluffy then add the anchovies and plenty of freshly ground black pepper. Spoon into a small serving dish and chill in the fridge before serving with a platter of raw vegetables such as pieces of carrot, baby corn, sweet peppers or cucumber alongside savoury biscuits.

SAUCE PIQUANTE

 (CHECK CONTENT OF MUSTARD)

* 3 tablespoons good-quality mayonnaise
* 1 teaspoon Dijon mustard
* 4 small cornichons (gherkins), finely chopped
* 1 teaspoon anchovy essence
* 1 tablespoon chopped chives or 4 spring onions, sliced

Mix all the ingredients together and serve with fried fish.

SAUCE TARTARE

* 1 shallot, finely chopped
* yolks from 2 hard-boiled eggs
* 1 tablespoon white wine vinegar
* 2 gherkins, finely chopped
* 1 heaped teaspoon capers, finely chopped
* 1 tablespoon parsley, finely chopped
* salt and freshly ground black pepper to taste

Fry the shallot in a little oil until soft and just beginning to turn brown. Put to one side to cool. Mash the egg yolks in a bowl and add a good amount of freshly ground black pepper and a pinch of salt. Gradually drop in the oil, beating all the time, and then gradually add the vinegar, mixing well. Beat the fried shallot to a pulp and add to the egg mixture. Mix in the gherkins, capers and parsley and serve with fried fish.

MARINADE FOR LAMB (LEG, SHOULDER, CHOPS OR CUTLETS) OR STEAK

* 2 tablespoons olive oil
* 1 tablespoon Worcestershire sauce
* juice 1 lemon
* 2 tablespoons soy
* 1 clove garlic, chopped
* freshly ground black pepper
* mixed handful herbs of your choice: thyme, rosemary, oregano, etc.

Mix all the ingredients and pour over the meat so that it is well covered. Leave in a cool place until ready to grill or roast.

PRAWN DIP

* 1 tablespoon horseradish sauce
* juice 1 lemon
* 1 tablespoon tomato ketchup
* 2 tablespoons mayonnaise
* 1 tablespoon crème fraîche

Whisk all the ingredients in a bowl until you have a smooth cream.

EGG SAUCE

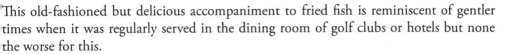

This old-fashioned but delicious accompaniment to fried fish is reminiscent of gentler times when it was regularly served in the dining room of golf clubs or hotels but none the worse for this.

* 2 hard-boiled eggs, roughly chopped
* 1 tablespoon roughly chopped parsley
* cayenne pepper

FOR THE WHITE SAUCE:

* 1 tablespoon butter
* 1 tablespoon flour
* 275ml milk
* salt and pepper

Make the white sauce by melting the butter with the flour, stirring for a minute before whisking in the milk to avoid any lumps. Bring gently to the boil and when thick, remove from the heat and season with salt and pepper. Fold in the chopped egg, parsley and cayenne and serve hot.

HOT LEMON DIP

This is great with barbecue chicken or sausages.

* 110g butter
* 4 level tablespoons flour
* 1 clove garlic, chopped
* ¼ teaspoon salt
* freshly ground black pepper
* ½ teaspoon dried thyme
* ½ teaspoon Tabasco
* zest 1 lemon and the juice of 2
* 150ml chicken stock

Melt the butter, add the garlic and stir in the flour. Cook for 2 minutes stirring all the while. Add all the remaining ingredients making sure there are no lumps (use a small whisk if this is the case). Bring to the boil, cover and simmer for 10 minutes. Pour into a bowl and allow to cool.

BREAKFAST AND LIGHT MEAL SUGGESTIONS

(V) (VG) (DF)   Mashed avocado with lemon juice, red chilli and fresh coriander piled on to a piece of mixed grain bread toasted and rubbed with garlic.

(V) (DF)   A few Swiss chard leaves picked in flurries of snow and steamed, served on top of a piece of multi-grain bread toasted with a scrambled egg pepped up with the first pickings of chive-like shoots from the potted shallots.

(V) (VG) (DF) (G)   Mushrooms sliced and cooked in their own juice piled onto a piece of toasted mixed grain bread.

(V) (VG) (DF) (G)   Salad of mixed microgreens, baby sorrel, baby salad leaves, pea shoots, little olive oil, balsamic vinegar, salt and freshly ground black pepper.

(V) (DF)   Omelette with cooked tomatoes and 1 slice mixed grain bread.

(V) (VG) (DF) (G)   Lettuce, asparagus and heirloom tomato salad with olive oil, lemon juice, mint and basil dressing.

PUDDINGS

Sometimes I wonder if it wouldn't be a good idea to start the meal with a pudding simply because, by the time we reach this stage in the proceedings, my appetite has dwindled. Having said that, usually I find a little space to accommodate something sweet.

QUICK CHOCOLATE TART

This recipe is not for you if you are practising girth control…

* 225g bar dark chocolate with 70% cocoa solids
* 275ml double cream
* 100ml Irish cream liqueur
* 1 ready-made, pre-cooked all-butter pastry case

Break the chocolate into small pieces into a bowl. Heat the cream and pour over the chocolate, stirring as it melts. Mix in the Irish cream liqueur and pour onto the pre-cooked pastry case. Chill in the fridge to set. Enjoy and repent at your leisure.

CHOCOLATE SAUCE

Instant smiles accompanied with vanilla ice cream.

For each serving:

* 1 tablespoon golden caster sugar
* 150ml water
* 90g bar dark chocolate, 70% cocoa solids

Warm the sugar and water in a pan until dissolved. Break the chocolate into a bowl and stir in the hot syrup until it has melted and blended together. Serve straight away.

RETRO LEMON AND ELDERFLOWER FLAN

V

* 8 digestive biscuits
* Heaped tablespoon butter (unsalted preferably but slightly salted is fine)
* For the lemony topping:
* juice and zest 2 unwaxed lemons
* 150ml double cream
* 1x 397g tin condensed milk
* 2 tablespoons elderflower cordial

Crush or blitz the biscuits, melt the butter and mix together. Line an 18cm flan ring or shallow, pretty dish by pushing the crumbs firmly to the sides and base. Beat the double cream with the condensed milk and add the lemon juice and zest, then the elderflower cordial. Pour on top of the biscuit base and put in the fridge for at least a couple of hours to enable it to set. When ready to serve, decorate with elderflowers (if still available) and some gratings of lemon zest.

I have tried this with dark chocolate digestives and it gives another dimension.

ORANGE TART

V

* 1 pack all-butter flaky pastry
* 100g melted butter
* 1 egg, well beaten
* zest and juice 1 orange – keep the zest separate
* zest and juice 1 lemon – keep the zest separate
* 4 tablespoons sugar

Preheat the oven to 180°C (fan). Line an 18cm flan ring with the pastry, prick with a fork and place a piece of baking parchment on top and then weigh it down either with ceramic baking beads or dried pulses/butter beans. Bake for 10 minutes then remove the parchment and beads. Bake for a further 5 minutes and remove from the oven. Whisk the egg with the melted butter, orange and lemon juice and sugar. Pour through a sieve onto the pastry case (this will remove any stringy bits) and scatter the zests. Bake on the middle shelf for about 15–20 minutes making sure the pastry is cooked and crisp. Serve at room temperature with crème fraîche.

CRUMBLE MIX

* 5 heaped tablespoons plain flour
* 2 tablespoons ground almonds
* 110g butter
* 2 tablespoons sugar

Whizz everything in a blender until it resembles breadcrumbs.

APPLE AND STRAWBERRY CRUMBLE

* 4 eating apples, peeled, cored and sliced
* 225g strawberries, hulled and cut in half (frozen ones are fine)
* 3 tablespoons sugar
* crumble mix as per the above

Preheat the oven to 180°C (fan). Place the apples in a baking dish and scatter over the strawberries and sugar. Spoon on the crumble mix and bake for about 25 minutes until the top is golden and the fruit cooked.

HOMEMADE YOGHURT

* 570ml full-fat, organic milk
* 3 tablespoons natural bio yoghurt
* a clean, wide-mouthed vacuum flask

In a non-stick pan heat the milk to the boil, stirring to prevent burning on the bottom. Reduce the heat to a shivering simmer and cook for about 15 minutes. During this time, the water content of the milk will evaporate and a skin will form. Continue stirring and then take off the heat. Wait until the milk is at blood temperature between 35°C and 47°C. Whisk the yoghurt into the milk, including any skin, pour into the vacuum flask and leave for at least 8 hours or overnight. When nearing the end, retain 3 tablespoons and make another batch. Often commercial yoghurt has a sour aftertaste but, the more you reproduce from your own culture, the more the natural sweetness increases.

STICKY TOFFEE PAVLOVA

V

* 3 egg whites
* 4 tablespoons caster sugar
* 3 level teaspoons cornflour
* 2 teaspoons vanilla extract
* 1 teaspoon instant coffee dissolved in 3 tablespoons warm water

Preheat the oven to 100°C (fan). Place all the ingredients in a squeaky clean bowl and whisk until you have glossy, stiff peaks. It doesn't look as though this will happen, but it will – I promise. Cover a baking tray with baking parchment and spoon on the meringue leaving a slight well in the middle. It doesn't have to be round – if a rectangular shape works better, then that's fine. Bake for an hour during which time it will take on a little colour. When cool and just before serving, prepare the topping:

FOR THE TOPPING:

* 2 or 3 bananas
* juice 1 lemon
* 3 tablespoons caster sugar for the caramel
* 275ml double cream, whipped

Slice the bananas and mix with the lemon juice. Spread the whipped cream onto the pavlova and scatter the bananas on top.

Now make the caramel:

Put the sugar in a heavy-bottomed pan with 3 tablespoons of water and place on a medium/high heat. DO NOT STIR or it will crystallise. The water will evaporate and the sugar begin to caramelise. At this point you can tip the pan to swirl the sugar to even the cooking. When it reaches a dark, golden colour (but not burned) drizzle it over the pavlova and serve at once.

BAKED BANANAS (1)

* 1 ripe banana per person
* juice 2 oranges
* juice ½ lemon
* 100ml liqueur of your choice: Cointreau, Grand Marnier, dark rum…
* 1 heaped tablespoon demerara sugar
* freshly grated nutmeg
* sprinkle cinnamon
* 25g butter

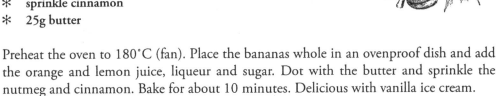

Preheat the oven to 180°C (fan). Place the bananas whole in an ovenproof dish and add the orange and lemon juice, liqueur and sugar. Dot with the butter and sprinkle the nutmeg and cinnamon. Bake for about 10 minutes. Delicious with vanilla ice cream.

BAKED BANANAS (2)

  & (IF USING MAPLE SYRUP)

* 1 banana per person
* juice 1 orange per 2 bananas
* juice ½ lemon per 2 bananas
* 1 tablespoon runny honey/maple syrup per 2 bananas
* sprinkle ground cinnamon
* a few gratings fresh nutmeg

Preheat the oven to 180°C (fan). Place the peeled bananas in a shallow ovenproof dish and add the other ingredients. Bake for about 10 minutes or until the fruit is cooked.

JUMBO ORGANIC PORRIDGE COOKED WITH STRAWBERRIES AND HONEY

  (IF USING MAPLE SYRUP INSTEAD OF HONEY)

FRESH PINEAPPLE AND BLUEBERRIES

KIWI FRUIT AND MANGO

RHUBARB STEWED WITH STRAWBERRIES AND A SLICE OF ROOT GINGER

191

MIXED FRUIT COMPOTE

* 2 peaches, peeled and sliced
* 200g black seedless grapes, halved
* 200g black cherries, stoned
* juice 2 oranges
* sugar to taste

Put everything into a pan and bring gently to the boil, stirring until the sugar has dissolved. Simmer for a few minutes until the juices run and the fruit is cooked but not to a mush. Cool, chill and serve.

INNOCENT ICE CREAM

* 400g strawberries (or any other soft fruit of your choice), hulled and cut in half
* 1 dessertspoon runny honey
* 500g full-fat natural yoghurt

Put the fruit into a blender and whizz. Add the honey and whizz again. Tip into a bowl and whisk in the yoghurt. Pour into an ice cream maker and proceed according to the manufacturer's instructions.

STRAWBERRY ALMOND SPONGE PUDDING

* 250g strawberries, hulled and cut in pieces to cover the bottom of an ovenproof dish
* 1 egg – weighed in its shell plus equal amounts of:
* sugar
* softened butter
* 50/50 self-raising flour and ground almonds

Preheat the oven to 180˚C (fan). Lay the strawberries on the bottom of the dish. Beat the sugar and butter with a handheld blender until soft and fluffy. Beat in the egg and then fold in the flour/almond mix. Carefully spoon over the fruit and bake for about 20 minutes or till golden and fluffed up.

AUTUMN PUDDING

This is an excellent way (instead of making banana bread) to use up those overripe bananas lurking in your fruit basket.

* 4 bananas
* about 2 heaped tablespoons blackberries (fresh or frozen)
* 1–2 tablespoons demerara sugar, according to taste
* juice 2 oranges
* 1 dessertspoon butter

Preheat the oven to 180˚C (fan). Peel the bananas and lay them in a shallow ovenproof dish. Scatter over the blackberries and pour on the orange juice. Sprinkle with the sugar and dot with the butter before placing in the oven for about 15 minutes. Serve warm as is, or with some crème fraîche, custard etc.

BANANA AND APPLE BAKED PUDDING

For 4–6

* 6 thin slices white bread, buttered
* 4–5 eating apples, peeled (put the peel to one side), cored and sliced
* 4 ripe bananas, peeled and sliced
* grated zest and juice 1 lemon
* 4 tablespoons demerara sugar
* caster sugar for dusting

Preheat the oven to 180°C (fan). Line a buttered, shallow pie dish with a mixture of apple and banana, sprinkle with lemon juice, zest and sugar and cover with thin slices of buttered bread. Repeat layers until the dish is full, ending up with buttered bread. Scatter the reserved apple peelings on top and bake until golden brown, approximately for 35–40 minutes. Discard the apple peelings and dust with the caster sugar before serving.

RASPBERRY YOGHURT ICE CREAM

* 500g raspberries
* 240g full-fat natural yoghurt
* juice ½ lemon
* 1 tablespoon caster sugar

If you have an ice cream maker, now is the time to use it. Whizz all the ingredients and pour gently into your machine. When frozen but not solid (a slightly sloppy consistency) pour/spoon into small containers and store in the freezer.

PEACHES IN ORANGE AND LEMON SYRUP

 V VG DF GF

* 2 peaches
* 4 tablespoons sugar
* 150ml water
* thinly peeled rind 1 orange and 1 lemon plus:
* juice of the lemon

Put the peaches in a bowl and pour over a kettle of boiling water. After a couple of minutes, drain and rinse under cold water. Peel off the skin, cut the fruit in half and remove the stones and put into a bowl. If they prove resistant, simply cut off the flesh around the stone with a knife. Put the sugar, water, lemon and orange peel into a pan and heat until the sugar has dissolved. Bring to the boil for 5 minutes so that the liquid has reduced by about a third. Remove from the heat and take out the peel. Add the lemon juice and pour over the peaches. Chi before serving.

FALLEN ANGEL PUDDING

V

For 6

* 6 plain chocolate digestive biscuits
* 25g unsalted butter, melted
* 150ml double cream
* 1x 397g tin condensed milk
* zest and juice 2 oranges
* juice 1 lemon
* 90g bar dark chocolate, 70% cocoa solids
* ramekins/coffee cups

Blitz the biscuits to a crumb and mix with the melted butter. Line the ramekins/cups with the mixture, pressing down to make a level base. Whisk the condensed milk and cream to blend. Add the orange zest and the orange and lemon juice. Pour on top of the biscuit base and chill in the fridge to set for a few hours. Before serving, grate some of the chocolate bar on top.

CHERRY ALMOND BAKED PUDDING

* 200g cherries
* 1 heaped tablespoon self-raising flour
* 1 tablespoon caster sugar plus a little extra
* 1 egg, beaten
* 55ml double cream
* 1 tablespoon ground almonds
* zest ½ lemon

Preheat the oven to 180°C (fan). Remove the stones from the cherries and scatter on the bottom of an ovenproof dish. In a bowl, mix all the other ingredients and pour over the fruit. Bake for about 30–40 minutes or until bubbling and lightly golden brown. Sprinkle with a dusting of caster sugar and serve warm or at room temperature with some double cream or ice cream.

CARAMELISED COMPOTE OF RHUBARB

* 500g rhubarb, cut into 3cm pieces
* 6 tablespoons sugar
* small glass water
* juice 1 lemon or orange

Put half the sugar (3 tablespoons) into a pan with the water and gently bring to the boil until the sugar caramelises. DON'T STIR or the sugar will turn to crystals. Do not let it burn – you are looking for a mid-to-dark brown colour. Remove from the heat and stir in the rhubarb, the remaining sugar and the orange/lemon juice. Place back on a medium heat and simmer gently until the fruit is cooked but not mushy – this will take about 8–10 minutes with careful watching. Serve chilled with custard, cream or ice cream.

EASY MANGO AND VANILLA ICE CREAM

* 500g luxury ready-made custard (check if gluten-free)
* 1 ripe mango
* 200ml crème fraîche
* 1 teaspoon vanilla extract

Peel the mango and cut off the flesh. Liquidise in a small food processor or use handheld blender. Mix the custard with the crème fraîche and vanilla extract using a hand whisk and fold in the mango purée. Pour into an ice cream maker and when ready, spoon into a plastic container with a lid and put in the freezer. Remove ¼ hour before eating so that it is soft enough to spoon into bowls.

CAKES

QUICK TEATIME TREAT

This is like falling off a log...

* 1 egg + same weight:
* self-raising flour
* sugar
* soft butter
* 1 dessertspoonful cocoa powder

Preheat the oven to 180°C (fan). Weigh the egg and then weigh equal amounts of self-raising flour, butter and sugar. Put everything in a bowl along with the cocoa powder and egg and incorporate using a handheld whisk. Alternatively, use a small blender. This takes seconds. Spoon the sponge mixture either into an 18cm cake tin or one for cupcakes. I have a tin for four small Yorkshire puddings and this works perfectly. Bake for about 6 minutes and test with a skewer. If it comes out clean they're done, if not cook a further minute or so. Cool in the tin for 5 minutes and then tip onto a wire cake rack. I like to ice these with an easy glacé icing.

GLACE ICING

* 3 tablespoons icing sugar
* 1 teaspoon instant coffee
* walnut pieces (optional)

Mix the instant coffee with a tablespoon of boiling water and beat into the icing sugar to a smooth paste. Spread immediately on the cooled cakes and decorate with the walnut pieces, if you have some to hand.

ANOTHER QUICK CAKE

* 1 egg + same weight:
* self-raising flour less one tablespoon
* soft butter
* sugar
* 1 tablespoon cocoa powder

FOR THE FILLING/TOPPING:

* good apricot jam
* 3 tablespoons icing sugar
* 1 tablespoon cocoa powder

Preheat the oven to 180°C (fan). Whisk everything together (except the topping) and pour into a buttered shallow 20cm cake tin. Bake on the middle shelf until a skewer comes out clean – about 10 minutes. When cool, cut in half across the cake to make 2 circles. Turn 1 over and spread liberally with the apricot jam and place the other half on top. Mix the cocoa powder and icing sugar together in a bowl and add a tablespoon of water to make a smooth, slightly runny icing. Spread over the cake and decorate with chocolate buttons or sprinkles or leave it plain.

FRUITY BUNS

* 1 egg + same weight:
* self-raising flour
* sugar
* soft butter
* zest and juice ½ lemon
* zest ½ orange
* 1 tablespoon sultanas or raisins

Preheat the oven to 180°C (fan). Whizz the egg, flour, sugar, butter, juice and zests together then fold in the dried fruit. Spoon into a muffin tin and bake till well risen and golden for about 8–10 minutes until the skewer comes out clean. Dust with a little caster sugar for extra crunch.

CAMPSITE GINGERBREAD

V

When we were children we headed for the Suffolk coast for our summer holidays either camping or borrowing Pa's lifelong friend's fisherman's hut alongside the River Blyth in Walberswick. Before we left home, Ma would make a huge batch of this simple gingerbread to take with us and, remarkably, it improved with age getting stickier as we neared the bottom of the old square tin in which it was always stored.

* 450g plain flour
* ½ teaspoon salt
* 2 tablespoons ground ginger
* 2 teaspoons baking powder
* ½ teaspoon bicarbonate of soda
* 8 tablespoons demerara sugar
* 175g butter
* 105g golden syrup
* 275ml milk
* 1 egg, beaten

Preheat the oven to 180°C (fan). Grease a shallow, non-stick baking tin (approx. 20cm x 20cm) – a square or rectangular one is ideal so that you can cut the gingerbread into fingers. Sieve all the dry ingredients except the sugar into a large bowl. Warm the sugar, butter and golden syrup on a low/medium heat until everything has melted. Warm the milk in a separate pan and combine with all the other ingredients, adding the beaten egg last. Pour into the prepared tin and bake for about 30 minutes or until a skewer comes out clean. When completely cold, cut into squares or rectangles and store in an airtight container. Best eaten around a camp fire.

INDEX

G

ABOUT THE AUTHOR

Coming from Sussex where **Bryony Hill** was also educated, after a year at Brighton College of Art, she spent four years in France after which, on returning to England, she met and eventually married the television sports presenter Jimmy Hill. Bryony has been busy in the kitchen for as long as she can remember and this, her eleventh book, is inspired by her mother who, with boundless patience, showed her how to weave baskets from cane, to make finger puppets from flour and water paste, and most importantly, to cook. Apart from writing and cooking, Bryony is a keen gardener and painter and many of her stunning, original artwork are available to purchase at www.bryonyhill.com

ALSO BY BRYONY HILL

A Compost Kind of Girl

Penalty Chick

Angel in an Apron

How I long to be with you – War Letters Home

My Gentleman Jim – a Love Story

Grow Happy, Cook Happy, Be Happy

Scotland to Shalimar – a Family's Life in India

An Indian Table – a Family's Recipes During the Raj

Artwork: www.bryonyhill.com

CHILDREN'S BOOKS

The Computer Lab

The Adventures of Silly Billy (written by Robin Whitcomb, illustrated by Bryony Hill)

Mr Teddy Gets a Job